PROGRESSIVELY WORSE

ALSO BY JOE CONCHA

Come On, Man! The Truth About Joe Biden's
Terrible, Horrible, No-Good, Very Bad Presidency

PROGRESSIVELY
WORSE

Why Today's Democrats
Ain't Your Daddy's Donkeys

JOE CONCHA

BROADSIDE BOOKS

HarperCollins books may be purchased for educational, business, or sales promotional use. For information, please email the Special Markets Department at SPsales@harpercollins.com.

Broadside Books™ and the Broadside logo are trademarks of HarperCollins Publishers.

FIRST EDITION

Designed by Michele Cameron

Library of Congress Cataloging-in-Publication Data

Names: Concha, Joe, author.
Title: Progressively worse : why today's Democrats
ain't your daddy's donkeys / Joe Concha.
Description: First edition. | New York :
HarperCollins Publishers, 2024. | Includes index. |
Identifiers: LCCN 2024011127 (print) | LCCN 2024011128 (ebook)
| ISBN 9780063334809 (hardcover) | ISBN 9780063334816 (ebook)
Subjects: LCSH: Democratic Party (U.S.) | Political culture—United States.
Classification: LCC JK2316 .C66 2024 (print) | LCC JK2316 (ebook)
| DDC 324.2736—dc23/eng/20240403
LC record available at https://lccn.loc.gov/2024011127
LC ebook record available at https://lccn.loc.gov/2024011128

24 25 26 27 28 LBC 5 4 3 2 1

To my wife, Jean, and kids, Cameron and Liam.
They're the only cheering section I need.

When you want to help people,
you tell them the truth. When you want to help yourself,
you tell them what they want to hear.

—THOMAS SOWELL

CONTENTS

PROGRESSIVELY
WORSE

How Did the Democratic Party
End Up So Far to the Left?
Here's One Theory. . . .

The big announcement came from CNN on August 27, 2019. Headline: CNN Announces Details for Climate Crisis Town Hall.

Premise: "Ten Democratic presidential hopefuls will appear in New York at back-to-back town halls on Wednesday, September 4, taking audience questions about their climate plans as scientists sound the alarm about global warming."

The event was scheduled to last (checks notes): *Seven hours.*

Boy, CNN really has its hand on the pulse of the people, doesn't it? Of all the issues facing the country at that time (and still to this day), *this* was what the network was going to give seven hours of consecutive airtime to when it comes to vetting Democratic presidential candidates.

But a look at a 2019 Pew Research poll, asking what respondents thought was the most important problem facing the country today, tells a much different story. Its annual survey that year showed that the economy was a top public priority for voters, as it always is. Health care, education, terrorism, and social security rounded out the top five. As for climate change, the issue CNN decided to blot out *420 minutes* of its regular programming for, it ranked *seventeenth* on the list of voter priorities, behind drug addiction, budget deficit, military, and transportation, among others.

Now, let's say you're a Democrat seeking the party nomination at that time. You look around and see that you're running against *twenty-six* other candidates, making getting your message/platform out extremely difficult, especially if you're not a top-tier candidate in polling. And then . . . a national news network says it's going to give you an hour alone onstage, along with a Wolf Blitzer or Anderson Cooper or Don Lemon, to make your case.

Do you take that offer? Of course you do. Because that kind of national airtime is scarce, and CNN does/did everything it can/could to appeal to Democrat voters.

But there is a catch: Maybe you want to talk about your economic and education proposals or dive into foreign policy. Ha! Are you kidding? CNN says the *climate crisis* is the only thing you're allowed to talk about.

Now, let's say you're a relative moderate running for president, like Steve Bullock, the Democratic governor of the red state of Montana. In order to win there statewide in his gubernatorial race, Bullock had to basically pose as a Republican. Donald Trump had won Montana by 20 points in 2016, after all, so no AOC-sounding progressive was going to sniff victory in John Dutton country. That's for certain.

Bullock does not support banning fracking, however. Ruh-roh, Shaggy. He also supported expansion of the Keystone XL pipeline. Oh, crap. That did not sit well with the moderators or much of the audience either. After all, these aren't dubbed climate change town halls, but *climate crisis* town halls.

Is this fearmongering on CNN's part? You bet. And the reason we know this is that Project Veritas had one of its reporters secretly tape a conversation with CNN technical director Charles Chester. And let's just say it tells us everything you need to know about journalism morphing into activism.

"Our focus was to get Trump out of office," Chester explained to

Veritas. "Without saying it, that's what it was, right? So our next thing is going to be for climate change awareness."

"Do you think it's going to be just like a lot of fear for the climate?" the undercover reporter asked.

"Yeah. Fear sells."

"Who decides that?"

"The head of the network," Chester replied.

The head of the network at that time was Jeff Zucker, who turned a once-respectable news organization into a progressive playpen that took far-left activist positions on things like the Climate Crisis.

From Zucker's perspective, CNN wasn't going to report on the world, it was going to *save* it. And it's not like it would be too hard to convince his "journalists" to come along for the mission. They were all fully on board, either because they also believed that becoming activists for liberal causes was in their job descriptions, or for the few that didn't think the Climate Crisis was a top priority to the country, they simply believed in the preservation of their careers.

CNN even went so far as to create the role of chief climate correspondent and handed it to Bill Weir, who has given us some rhetorical gems over the years.

Here's Weir on Republicans voting against the hilariously named Inflation Reduction Act: "Not a single Republican in either chamber voted for the first piece of ambitious climate legislation in U.S. history. Best case, they let their opponents become the party of Industrial Revolution 2.0. Worst case, their obstruction hastens the end of a livable Earth."

Here's Weir to Fox Nation after it produced a documentary on Al Gore and all of the wrong climate change apocalyptic predictions he's made over the years:

"Weather is not climate, you willfully ignorant fucksticks."

This guy just oozes Murrow and Cronkite, doesn't he?

Here's Weir to Sen. Joe Manchin (D-WV) after he announced he would not support a climate tax provision pushed by his party on Capitol Hill:

"This is hung up on an old-fashioned filibuster, sort of recent, made-up American rules, where the fate of life on Earth is at stake and doesn't seem to match."

There are dozens of other examples of just how hysterical this climate-porn dealer with a microphone is, but we only have so much room in this chapter. Besides, you get the idea: *this* is a person CNN decided to head up its reportage of environmental issues.

So are Democrats still the party for the little guy, the small business owner? Here's one big example why they aren't:

Rudford's Restaurant, San Diego. The popular twenty-four-hour diner has been in business since 1949. Remember, the restaurant business struggled enough during the lockdowns for months on end during the pandemic. Thousands of restaurants and eateries across the country did not even survive. But Democratic leaders, knowing most of the media will have their backs when it comes to shutting down pipelines, canceling offshore drilling, and banning fracking, all in the name of the Climate Crisis, simply do not care about the plight of restaurant owners, their employees, or their customers.

Rudford's is owned by brothers Jeff and Nick Kacha. In December 2022 its natural gas bill was $2,200. In January 2023, just the next month, it jumped to $8,200, *a 400 percent surge*. The electric bill, which was $2,000 before Covid, has now jumped to $5,000, or 250 percent.

"I think [California leadership] are trying to run us out of here," Jeff Kacha told *Fox & Friends First* at the time. "It's out of control. The costs are out of control."

"They're not exactly representing the people here in San Diego, I can tell you that," Nick Kacha added. "It just seems like they're throwing businesses under the bus. . . . We bring in so much tax revenue and everything for the city of San Diego. And they're here like stabbing us in the back almost with all these costs. It's sad to see . . . the people are suffering.

"There's just people that say they can't afford their bills any longer," he continued. "These are the people that need it most, and . . . it just doesn't seem like they're representing any of us."

When it comes to battling the Climate Crisis, always follow the money. But the bucks mostly stop when it comes to the leading polluters on the planet (China, India, Russia) and their contributions, all while the United States spends more of its already out-of-control budgets on this front. Note: India and China alone are responsible for nearly *one-third* of the world's emissions. So until they come on board—and that ain't happening except in the pipe dreams of John Kerry—the United States will bankrupt itself for no apparent reason.

Back to the 2019 primary season: a confused and irritated Joe Biden was struggling as a candidate. It's easy to see why: he's a terrible public speaker. He often yells in debate situations for no apparent reason. And he just looks and sounds so damn old.

But lest anyone think I think eightysomething is too old, because for many it's not, Biden is in that other category. To quote Indiana Jones, "It's not the years, honey. It's the mileage."

"Play the radio, make sure the television, excuse me, make sure you have a record player on at night!" Biden oddly yelled during a September 2019 primary debate, not realizing record players haven't been a common thing in households in decades. "Make sure that kids hear words, a kid coming from a very poor school, or a very poor background, will hear four million fewer words spoken by the time they get there."

WT(actual)F???

At the time, it was hard to envision such a woke party nominating an old white guy who once was the biggest champion of the 1994 crime bill and supported hundreds of miles of border fence, but it happened anyway. Note: No administration, including Trump's, has ever deported more illegals than Obama-Biden's (more on this later in the book). So when Biden made yet another run for president in 2019–20, the left was highly skeptical of their nominee.

Joe had to pivot to the left. And hard. So when CNN asked him during a town hall if he would ban fossil fuels and end drilling on federal lands, the geriatric showed the backbone of a jellyfish.

"No more subsidies for the fossil fuel industry!" Biden declared. "No more drilling on federal lands! No more drilling, including offshore! No ability for the oil industry to continue to drill, period!"

CNN's New York audience predictably applauded. And behind the scenes, network executives and its chief climate correspondent likely chest-bumped each other in a corner office overlooking Central Park.

And both CNN's and MSNBC's efforts would also hold single-topic presidential primary town halls. But not on US-China policy or sanctuary cities or fentanyl overdoses or America's failing schools, but on the Climate Crisis. And it made for glowing headlines from the usual suspects:

Washington Post: *"Four Big Takeaways from the MSNBC Climate Change Town Hall"*

New York Times: *"Environmental Justice Was a Climate Forum Theme. Here's Why"*

NBC News: *"Democrats Need to Take Climate Change Seriously. Appearing on the CNN Town Halls Was a Good Start"*

Speaking of NBC News, that sound you may hear from time to time is the late, great Tim Russert rolling over in his grave. Because Chuck Todd, who moderated *Meet the Press* throughout the Trump years, is not the objective, tough professional journalist whom both sides respected and often appeared with. Instead, Chuck proved to be another activist sitting high on a moral pedestal, there not to inform viewers but to *lecture them*.

"I know there's a lot of folks who think that, due to climate change and due to the globalization in general, it is inevitable that we'll deal with more and more viruses like this," Todd insisted in a conversation with Dr. Anthony Fauci in March 2021.

Hmmm. What folks, Chuck? And if Covid escaped from a lab in

China, which most sane and sensible people have concluded, what role exactly did climate change play? On this front, Jon Stewart, who at last check is quite liberal and therefore not pushing some right-wing talking point, explained the logic this way to a shocked Stephen Colbert one night on his CBS "comedy" program.

"'Oh, my God, there's a novel respiratory coronavirus overtaking Wuhan, China. What do we do?' 'Oh, you know who we could ask? The Wuhan novel respiratory coronavirus lab.' The disease is the same name as the lab. That's just a little too weird, don't you think?"

Colbert, taken off guard, tried to stop his old friend, but Stewart was rolling.

"Oh, my God, there's been an outbreak of chocolaty goodness near Hershey, Pennsylvania! What do you think happened? Like, 'Oh I don't know, maybe a steam shovel mated with a cocoa bean?' Or it's *the fucking chocolate factory*! Maybe that's it!"

Greatest analogy ever. Colbert, of course, responded by asking if Stewart had been hanging out with Republican senators lately in coming to such a conclusion. Lame.

But Chuck Todd believes climate change somehow is a key element in producing coronaviruses. He also once vowed to make climate change a big issue on his weekly Sunday show while banning all "climate deniers" from appearing on his program.

"We're not going to debate climate change, the existence of it," Todd said in December 2018. "The earth is getting hotter and human activity is a major cause. Period!"

As you'll see as a recurring theme throughout this book, always judge a politician or "journalist" on actions, not words. On cue, Todd was cheered by almost everyone in the press for making his emphatic statement.

But then a funny thing happened in the months following his climate oration.

"Since Todd's admirable, single-focus segment, climate change has gone almost completely missing from *Meet the Press* broadcasts," a July

2019 story on Mediaite reads. "A survey of its shows from January through June found less than 10 minutes of discussion about the topic out of the nearly 1,000 minutes of Sunday morning airtime, or just one percent of the total. Likewise, Todd hasn't interviewed a single climate scientist about the issue since December, despite numerous newsworthy Washington moments and natural disasters explicitly related to the topic."

Wow. This book really does write itself. Oh, and as for that ban on climate deniers appearing on his program, here's what Sen. Ron Johnson (R-WI) had to say on the matter.

"I don't know about you guys, but I think climate change is—as Lord Monckton said—bullshit," Johnson reportedly told a Republican group in July 2021, per CNN.

A few months later, Todd hosted that very same climate change denier Johnson on his program. So much for the ban. And here's the best part: neither the Climate Crisis nor any other discussion of the environment was broached during Todd's extensive interview of Johnson. *Not. Once.*

But Chuck did get quite upset when Johnson broached media bias and social media censorship of conservatives.

"Look, you can go back on your partisan cable cocoon and talk about media bias all you want. I understand it's part of your identity," Todd said piously to the senator.

Yup, no bias there whatsoever. And such professionalism!

Tim Russert. We miss you, buddy.

As a media and political observer, Bill Maher is the commonsense guy in the party on more than a few issues these days. He also is unafraid to call out members of his own party.

"My name is Bill, and I fly private," Maher said during his closing monologue during one show in January 2023. "And so does every other person who calls themselves an 'environmentalist' who can!"

"Everyone else is full of shit and I'm done being full of shit," Maher said after showing photos of Leonardo DiCaprio, George Clooney, Brad Pitt, Oprah Winfrey, Bono, Mark Zuckerberg, Beyoncé and Jay-Z, the

Clintons, and Senators Bernie Sanders (I-VT) and Elizabeth Warren (D-MA), all flying private.

"I can take being a bad environmentalist because almost all of us are, but I can't take being a hypocrite," Maher continued. "Now, I always justified renting a plane because I only used it for work and literally could not get to most of my stand-up gigs on time any other way. How do you think I did it all those years I said good night here at 8 pm and was onstage in Vegas at 10? But I don't need to do stand-up, like tomorrow night in Albuquerque. And outside of heads of state, almost everyone else *could* fly commercial. Why don't they? Ask anyone who tried to get home for Christmas last year. . . ."

"People take jets to environmental conferences!" Maher continued. "If you could run TED Talks on hypocrisy, you wouldn't need coal. Look, sorry not sorry. I tried to do my part to the environment. I never had kids, the one thing worse for the planet than private jets . . . I had the first-generation Prius in 2001. It looked like a Tylenol gel cap. I was always handing my keys to valets that were driving a better car than me. I had the first Tesla in 2010. And honestly, both these cars sucked. . . . But both times, I said to myself, 'Okay, I'll take one for the team because I have a platform, so I'll do the right thing. And then everybody will follow.' . . . Nobody followed."

This is so correct. And I can tell you that most of the people you see on cable news get car services to and from their homes to the studio, including me. And these aren't Priuses being sent, but usually a gas-guzzling Cadillac Escalade or Chevy Suburban the size of my old apartment in Hoboken, because professional car services in New York aren't going to send a Honda Civic. Also note: You could send a moped for me in Jersey and I wouldn't care, as long as I can work while commuting with a laptop up. But know this: almost nobody in this business who is on the air is taking a train to work to save the environment.

Don't expect much to change during the presidential debates going into the general election in 2024, either. Just look back to 2020 as the playbook: NBC's Kristen Welker was chosen to moderate the second and final debate between Trump and Biden. And here are the topics she chose:

» Fighting COVID-19
» American families
» Race in America
» The Climate Crisis
» National security
» Leadership

And here were the most important issues to American voters in 2020 per Gallup:

1. Health care (Welker omitted)
2. Terrorism and national security (Welker included)
3. Gun policy (Welker omitted)
4. Education (Welker omitted)
5. The economy (Welker omitted)
6. Immigration (Welker omitted)

Of course, the Climate Crisis made the cut. It made Joe Biden look noble as he talks about ending the Keystone XL pipeline. Making climate a central theme means that Trump gets portrayed as uncaring and aloof in pushing for continued American energy independence while the planet allegedly marches toward its end.

And the clock is ticking, according to Rep. Alexandria Ocasio-Cortez, a media goddess if one ever existed.

"Millennials and people, you know, Gen Z and all these folks that will come after us, are looking up and we're like: 'The world is gonna end in 12 years if we don't address climate change, and your biggest issue is how are we gonna pay for it?'" she once asked in January 2019.

That means we have (checks notes) just seven years left. *Seven*. I've never even been to the Masters or the Kentucky Derby. Man, this sucks.

Or maybe, *just maybe*, we'll be around a lot longer. Before AOC, in 2009 at the Copenhagen climate change crisis, there was Al Gore saying things like this:

"These figures are fresh. Some of the models suggest to Dr. [Wieslav] Maslowski that there is a 75 percent chance that the entire north polar ice cap, during the summer months, could be completely ice-free within five to seven years."

Hmmm . . . that means we should have seen the end of the polar ice cap in 2016. Seas rising by such a huge amount, according to actual scientists, would mean that every coastal city on the planet would be completely flooded and destroyed.

At last check, that hasn't happened. But don't expect almost anyone in the US media to call Gore or AOC or Kerry or Biden out.

Because, as that CNN director said to Project Veritas, *fear sells*. And no one exploits it better to scare its largely mis- or underinformed voters than the donkey party.

It makes one yearn for a time when Democratic leaders used to be grounded in some semblance of reality and principle. A time when John F. Kennedy came into office facing a recession and turned everything around by going full Reagan in advocating tax cuts, beefing up America's military, and opposing racial quotas.

And, yes, for you younger readers, this kind of Democrat actually existed. . . .

PART I

Remember When Democrats Cared about Democracy?

In a democracy, every citizen, regardless of his interest in politics, "holds office"; every one of us is in a position of responsibility; and, in the final analysis, the kind of government we get depends upon how we fulfill those responsibilities. We, the people, are the boss, and we will get the kind of political leadership, be it good or bad, that we demand and deserve.

—JOHN F. KENNEDY

But while the threat to American democracy is real, I want to say as clearly as we can: We are not powerless in the face of these threats. We are not bystanders in this ongoing attack on democracy. There are far more Americans—far more Americans from every—from every background and belief who reject the extreme MAGA ideology than those that accept it. And, folks, it is within our power, it's in our hands—yours and mine—to stop the assault on American democracy.

—JOSEPH R. BIDEN

Here we have one Democrat who speaks of democracy as a call to action to every American citizen.

Democracy, he argues from a macro perspective, is what each and every one of us puts into it, regardless of political stripe. The responsibility of preserving and protecting it depends on We the People.

At least, that's how I read JFK's remarks.

On the other hand, here we have another Democrat president who uses democracy as the tip of a spear against his political opponents. He calls them "extreme." He believes they wish to attack democracy and threaten the whole country. And apparently, he and his supporters are the only ones who can "stop the assault on American democracy."

Democrats today use impeachment strictly for made-for-TV theater. They threaten to blow up the Constitution by expanding the courts and to keep their opponents off state ballots. They weaponize the justice system to jail their competition before elections.

Today's Democrats are—and it ain't even close—the biggest threat to democracy today. This perspective is based on their actions, which are profoundly and patently un-American.

So buckle up as our first section explores all of this, with a little humor thrown in to avoid completely depressing you. Besides, when we're talking about Hunter Biden and Joe Biden and Kamala Harris, how can one possibly avoid the comedy of it all?

CHAPTER 1

That Sexist, Racist Constitution!

The poll from Rasmussen Reports says it all about the mindset of Democrats these days:

"Fifty-seven percent of Democratic voters agree it 'is a document rooted in racism,' and 64% think the Constitution 'is a sexist document that gives men advantages over women.' Nearly half (49%) of Democrats believe the Constitution 'should be mostly or completely rewritten.'"

Sexist! Racist! Just throw the thing out and start all over!

We hear *a lot* from the media about what a threat MAGA Republicans are to democracy. But at last check, those folks don't want to tear up the Constitution. They also don't want their presidents acting like autocrats. This argument isn't better evidenced than by what we're seeing from donkeys in the US Congress.

The time was late June 2023, and the 1-2-3 haymakers leveled by the Supreme Court against the liberal establishment measured high on the political Richter scale.

Affirmative action? Dead.

Student loan forgiveness? Dead.

First Amendment rights for store owners? Alive and well!

In reacting to these decisions, the meltdowns by many in the media and Democratic lawmakers were unhinged on steroids. On cue, we heard talk again of expanding the Supreme Court, which would obviously be weaponized by whichever party is in power.

"People don't have to live under constant fear of the Supreme Court. We can't sit on our hands while these justices carry out the bidding of right wing organizations," wrote Sen. Tina Smith (D-MN) in June 2023. "Expand the Court."

"Everything should be on the table: reform and expansion," Rep. Ayanna Pressley (D-MA) told MSNBC at the time.

The questions asked by those on cable news have only thrown kerosene on this fire. Former Obama "Green Czar" and current CNN host Van Jones called the Supreme Court "my enemy" while waxing poetic thusly:

"The younger generation's values are being rubbed in the dog poo by the Supreme Court over and over again," he declared on national television. Print media also went all in on attacking the decisions, led by the *Washington Post*.

"The Supreme Court Can Save Itself from the Crisis the Justices Created," a headline by the paper's editorial board decreed in a piece that called for term limits for Supreme Court members, a position that the paper oddly didn't feel compelled to share when the Court was more liberal than conservative.

So are Democrats and their allies in the media representing what America's thinking on these recent SCOTUS decisions? Nope. Not even close.

Take an ABC News/Ipsos poll at the time as an example of the disconnect when it comes to affirmative action. More than half of American voters, 52 percent, approved of the high court's decision on restricting the use of race as a factor in college admissions, while just 32 percent disapproved. For independent voters, the number approving jumped to 58 percent. And for Asian voters (because Asian students are the most negatively impacted by affirmative action), the number was the same: 58 percent approval.

On the ruling surrounding student loan forgiveness, a plurality gave a thumbs-up to the decision to strike down President Biden's gambit, with 45 percent approving and 40 percent disapproving. The rest (15 percent) said they weren't sure. And on the decision to allow an evangelical Christian website designer to refuse to serve LGBTQ+ customers under First Amendment rights, voters were evenly split: 40 percent approving, 40 percent disapproving.

But if you watched and read the coverage that June, you could only conclude that 90 percent of the country was against the Supreme Court on *all* of these issues. Clearly that wasn't the case.

But then something truly odd, even for Congress, began rearing its ugly head: multiple members of Congress began calling the very body they represent practically irrelevant, advocating that the chamber be usurped in favor of the president acting unilaterally, like a king, if he wanted to, say . . . declare that hundreds of millions of dollars in student loans be forgiven.*

As for Congress, who needs it? But the Founding Fathers were quite clear when they decreed that Congress controls the purse strings of American taxpayer money. No matter: we heard Dem lawmakers openly saying they wanted *themselves* taken out of the equation, along with the Senate, thereby advocating that the president should simply make and pass laws as he deems fit.

If this scenario sounds like democracy dying in dictatorship, it's because it's *exactly that*. This kind of support for absolute power by one-third of the government (the executive branch) is literally the definition of antidemocracy authoritarianism.

Need proof? Here's what Alexandria Ocasio-Cortez told CNN at the time:

"These are the types of rulings that signal a dangerous creep towards authoritarianism and centralization of power in the court," she warned.

---

* Sydney Lake, "AOC Presses Biden to Use Executive Power to Wipe Out Student Loan Debt," *Fortune*, November 30, 2021, https://fortune.com/education/articles/aoc-presses-biden-to-use-executive-power-to-wipe-out-student-loan-debt/.

Again, if you're keeping score at home, here you have the most popular Democratic member of Congress (on social media, anyway) openly supporting absolute power for the executive branch. After the Supreme Court ruling, ninety Democrat lawmakers urged Biden in an open letter to ignore the ruling, ignore Congress, and just use his executive tools to forgive the loans anyway. So here's AOC saying that *the Supreme Court*, which rightly argued in the majority opinion that the president has a constitutional obligation to go to Congress first, is the branch of the government creeping toward authoritarianism.

Rep. Ro Khanna (D-CA), who is supposed to be one of the more moderate Democrats, made a similar argument to ABC's Jonathan Karl at the time: the Supreme Court, she said, "shouldn't be overturning the will of Congress just because they think Congress gave too much power to the president." Again, Congress had *zero say* in Biden's loan program, so what "will" exactly is the congressman talking about?

"Republican hypocrisy on student loan forgiveness is astounding," tweeted the censured Adam Schiff (D-CA). "The same politicians that were happy to take millions in PPP loans think young people should be left mired in debt." Schiff is knowingly ignoring one inconvenient fact: the 2020 PPP loans *were passed by Congress* and signed into law by President Trump, and therefore implemented the legal way legislatively. Biden's student loan gambit, conversely, avoided Congress entirely.

Enter CBS News, in what was somehow billed a straight news story and not an opinion piece: "PPP Loans Cost Nearly Double What Biden's Student Debt Forgiveness Would Have. Here's How the Programs Compare."

The whole pesky nugget around the need for Congress to pass legislation into law wasn't broached. Other outlets followed suit.

There's no shortage of hypocrisy in Washington. It's just so blatant, and since we have a media too lazy to do the homework to call out those who engage in it, it will continue in perpetuity.

Here's a fine example: Joe Biden in 2008 evoking the unitary executive, which greatly expands the power and reach of the executive branch. "Vice President Cheney has been the most dangerous vice president we've had probably in American history," Biden bellowed during a vice presidential debate with Sarah Palin. "The idea he doesn't realize is that Article I of the Constitution defines the role of the vice president of the United States, that's the Executive Branch. He works in the Executive Branch. He should understand that. Everyone should understand that. . . . The idea he's part of the Legislative Branch is a bizarre notion invented by Cheney to aggrandize the power of a unitary executive and look where it has gotten us. It has been very dangerous."

Got it. So surely when Biden took office in January 2021, he would live up to his words regarding the whole not-aggrandize-the-power-of-the-unitary-executive thing, correct? Of course not. In Biden's first hundred days alone, he signed off on 106 executive actions, or more than one per day on average. That's more than Trump. That's more than Obama. That's more than Bush, whose vice president was apparently the most dangerous in history.

Republicans (barely) took back control of the House in 2022, and suddenly, almost like magic, Democrats and especially Biden do not care about the dangers of the unitary executive, which I'm naming my fantasy football team after next year.

Expand the Court! Tear up the Constitution! Congress? Who needs 'em?

These definitely are not your daddy's donkeys anymore.

CHAPTER 2

The Original Election Deniers . . .

The US presidential election result was utterly shocking to the party nominee with huge name recognition. Said nominee truly believed there was no way defeat was possible.

After the votes were tallied and a winner was declared, the nominee's allies immediately blamed the loss not on the candidate or campaign strategy but instead on the election being "hacked." Many media organizations echoed this claim, pointing to the candidate underperforming in counties that used voting machines instead of paper ballots as proof.*

"Vladimir Putin himself directed the covert cyberattacks against our electoral system, against our democracy, apparently because he has a personal beef against me," the aforementioned nominee, Hillary Clinton, said five weeks before her opponent, Donald Trump, was sworn in. "This is an attack against our country," she went on. "We are well beyond normal political concerns here. This is about the integrity of our democracy and the security of our nation."

There was no ambiguity from Clinton in the weeks following the

---

* Dan Merica, "Computer Scientists Urge Clinton Campaign to Challenge Election Results," CNN, November 23, 2016, https://www.cnn.com/2016/11/22/politics /hillary-clinton-challenge-results/index.html.

2016 election: Trump won because of Russia and "covert cyberattacks against our electoral system." Democrats, along with many political commentators, echoed Clinton's sentiment: the Kremlin installed Trump, and did so through nefarious cyber means.

The drumbeat in the media followed for three years as Special Counsel Robert Mueller's Russia investigation dragged on. And the term *hacked* continued to be used in headlines as it pertained to Russia and Trump's victory.

Per *Merriam-Webster*: "**Hack:** to gain illegal access to (a computer network, system, etc.)"*

"Every day there are new developments, new shoes dropping, so to speak, that call into question the legitimacy of his win," Clinton campaign spokesperson Brian Fallon said of President-elect Trump on CNN on January 13, 2016.†

Politico magazine went even further: "Make no mistake: Hacking the 2016 election was an act of war. It's time we responded accordingly."‡

This sentiment, presented without evidence, had a profound effect on Democratic voters' perception of the 2016 election. A 2018 YouGov poll, for example, found that more than *two-thirds* of Democratic voters believed Russia changed vote totals away from Clinton and over to Trump.

Also in 2018, Democrats on Capitol Hill declared on the House floor that there was absolutely no doubt that voting machines could be hacked and vote totals could be changed. This wasn't some cable news

---

* *Merriam-Webster*, s.v. "hack," https://www.merriam-webster.com/dictionary/hack.

† Mark Hensch, "Ex-Clinton aide: Trump 'very insecure' about legitimacy," *The Hill*, January 13, 2017, https://thehill.com/homenews/administration/314223-ex-clinton-aide-trump-very-insecure-on-legitimacy/.

‡ Mark Hertling and Molly K. McKew, "Putin's Attack on the U.S. Is Our Pearl Harbor," *Politico*, July 16, 2018, https://www.politico.com/magazine/story/2018/07/16/putin-russia-trump-2016-pearl-harbor-219015/.

segment with allies of a candidate, but comments made by lawmakers, entered into the record and broadcast nationally on C-SPAN.

Sen. Ron Wyden (D-OR): *"The biggest seller of voting machines is doing something that violates Cybersecurity 101 by directly installing remote access software which would make a machine like that a magnet for fraudsters and hackers."*

Rep. Jennifer Wexton (D-VA): *"In 2018 electronic voting machines in Georgia and Texas deleted votes for certain candidates or switched votes from one candidate to another."*

Sen. Kamala Harris (D-CA): *"I actually held a demonstration for my colleagues where we brought in folks who before our eyes hacked machines that are being used in many states."*

Rep. Ted Lieu (D-CA): *"Workers were able to easily hack into electronic voting machines to switch votes. In a close presidential election they just need to hack one swing state or maybe one or two, or maybe just a few counties in one swing state."*

There are *dozens* of other quotes that mirror the ones you just read. So which is it? Can these machines be hacked or not? Democrats also made the same claims on CNN and MSNBC, yet no massive lawsuit came about. I wonder why that is. (Actually, I don't wonder at all.)*

Now let's look at the 2020 presidential election. A raging pandemic meant mail-in ballots would be used by voters in unprecedented numbers. And if you recall, Donald Trump led Joe Biden in several key

---

* Tom Rogan, "Whoever Convinced Most Democrats That Putin Hacked the Election Tallies Is Doing Putin's Bidding," *Washington Examiner*, November 19, 2018, https://www.washingtonexaminer.com/opinion/whoever-convinced-most -democrats-that-putin-hacked-the-election-tallies-is-doing-putins-bidding.

states on Election Day, including Pennsylvania, Georgia, Wisconsin, and Michigan. If Trump won three of those four states, he would have won again.

But as mail-in votes were counted for several days after Election Day, all of those states flipped to Joe Biden. The former vice president was officially declared the winner four days after Election Day as a result. Trump and his legal team cried foul, claiming the candidate was robbed and his opponent's victory illegitimate.

Sound familiar?

Dozens of lawsuits were filed on behalf of Trump across several states, including Pennsylvania, Georgia, and Michigan, just one day after Election Day. Those lawsuits would all eventually fail.

Just as in 2016 after that presidential election, the 2020 election was contested by a losing candidate and by his allies by saying the results were not legitimate. In 2016 and 2017, news organizations booked allies and members of the Clinton camp to discuss and inquire about those claims.

Two years after the 2020 election, just as YouGov had in 2018, Monmouth University ran a poll asking Republican voters if Biden's win was legitimate. And similar to YouGov's findings but with the shoe on the other foot, nearly two-thirds of GOP voters thought the losing candidate was robbed despite no evidence of fraud existing.

As we entered 2024, Joe Biden's age and performance had Democrats and the media extremely worried. Bigly. So the thought process was right out of the Kremlin: if you can't beat Trump, simply take away citizens' ability to vote for him. And on cue, a few Democratic judges in Colorado decided without any Republican input to take Trump off the ballot in that state by arguing that he had incited insurrection, even though he was never charged with doing so. The state of Maine quickly followed, courtesy of a unilateral decision by one Maine secretary of state (Shenna Bellows) using the same ridiculous reason. This is election interference, plain and simple. But Democrats don't care about anything but power and winning by any means possible, even if it means trying to defeat Trump by forfeit instead of on the issues.

Fortunately for sanity, the Supreme Court rightly ruled in March 2024 that Colorado cannot take Trump off the ballot. Instead, the 9–0 ruling states, such a move can be carried out only by Congress. Imagine that: allowing voters instead of judges or rogue state secretaries to decide who wins or loses elections. Democrats *way* overplayed their hand here, and it only supercharged Trump's campaign, because once again he was proved right regarding the Blue Team abusing the justice system in an effort to defeat him.

The party also overplayed its hand in Fulton County, Georgia, in attempting to try a RICO case against Trump, arguing that he attempted to steal the election in the Peach State. The district attorney in charge of the case, Fani Willis, thought it was a great idea to hire her married boyfriend, Nathan Wade, to be lead prosecutor and even compensated him more than $600,000 for the effort. Wade was the Atlanta version of *Better Call Saul*, basically playing an ambulance chaser during his career and therefore had never tried a federal case like the one against Trump.

It was eventually revealed that Wade had taken Willis on multiple vacations to expensive places like Napa, on two Caribbean cruises, and on Florida getaways, allegedly with the money Willis was paying him. For her part, she denied the allegations. But texts proved otherwise, and a Fulton County judge ruled in March 2024 that either Fani had to excuse herself from the Trump case or Wade needed to go. The latter option was quickly taken, allowing Fani to stay on the case.

But the damage was done. The AG is toxic. Damaged goods. Her credibility shot. Democrats thought they could beat Trump through a lawfare approach, but the whole effort was quickly dissolving while Trump's numbers continued to rise as winter became spring in 2024.

As we head toward Election Day, one thing is certain: whichever side loses won't accept defeat graciously. If Trump wins, we'll hear about the end of democracy and "conservative media" pushing him over the finish line in key swing states that exist mostly in the Midwest (Pennsylvania, Michigan, Wisconsin, Ohio) and Southwest (Arizona and Nevada). We're also hearing that many Democrats are now saying that if Trump wins, they will vote against certifying him because they view him as ineligible. Uh-huh. And if Democrats win, Republicans/conservatives will point to mail-in voting and not having an all-paper-ballots system as the reason that they lost.

Either way, a good chunk of the country will have zero faith we can have free and fair national elections. And that ain't a good thing. So here's my proposal:

Let's get rid of electronic voting machines.

Let's go back to paper ballots only.

Let's make Election Day a national holiday and move it to a Monday (three-day weekend!).

Let's allow for mail-in voting, but only for two weeks prior, and only if you're in active military or over the age of seventy.

And finally, in urban areas where long lines have existed in the past, let's invest millions in creating mobile voting sites in the most congested areas to make sure it's a relatively easy process for all.

That's commonsense stuff. But Democrats on Capitol Hill will never allow this to happen. The only way it will happen is if Republicans have control of the House, Senate, and White House. Otherwise, Democrats will block any effort to allow for an orderly and sane process.

And while we're on the subject of common sense, you'll never guess which political TV host and comedian has become the voice of reason of the Democratic Party. . . .

CHAPTER 3

Bill Maher

The Dems' Voice of Reason?

How far to the left has the Democratic Party gone? Bill Maher is now the commonsense face of the party.

Yes, yes . . . I hear you. He's said some profoundly nasty stuff about Trump. He called Sarah Palin the C-word. He even once donated $1 million to Barack Obama's reelection campaign. So I'm not saying he'll be speaking at your average Turning Point USA summit or CPAC anytime soon. I'm not implying he'll ever vote Republican.

But if you listen to Maher speak lately, it's hard to disagree with his perspective. And what I like about the HBO host more than anything is this: unlike all of the phonies in this business that won't dare deviate from a narrative their audiences are comfortable with, all out of fear of getting nasty-grams from those audiences and readers, Maher honestly doesn't give a shit if other liberals in the media or in his audience are offended by what he has to say.

To that end, I've compiled the top ten Bill Maher quotes since Biden took office, per Grabien, a multimedia marketplace that transcribes political programs and provides highlight clips:

10. June 12, 2021: "The *Friends* reunion we just had looked weird, because if you even suggested a show today about six people all of whom were straight and white, the network would laugh you out of the room and then cancel you on Twitter. And yet there is a recurrent theme on the far left that things have never been worse."

9. March 13, 2021: "Do you know who doesn't care that there's a stereotype of a Chinese man in a Dr. Seuss book? China. All 1.4 billion of them couldn't give a crouching tiger flying fuck, because they're not a silly people. If anything, they are as serious as a prison fight."

8. June 12, 2021: "There are a helluva lot of Americans trying really hard these days to create a new spirit of inclusion and self-reflection, and this progressive allergy to acknowledging societal advances is self-defeating. . . . Having a warped view of reality leads to policies that are warped Blacks-only dorms and graduation ceremonies, a growing belief in whiteness as a malady and [that] white people are irredeemable. Giving up on a colorblind society—only if you believe we've made no progress does any of that make sense."

7. September 3, 2023: "Murders have been happening in Chicago among the African American community for far too long and not really reported in the way they should be. It's amazing how Black lives don't seem to matter when they are taken by Black lives."

6. April 22, 2023: "Why aren't there, you know, a hundred giant Black celebrities who would have the respect of those people saying, 'What are you doing to yourself, why are you killing each other?'"

5. April 22, 2023: "We already spend a lot of money on schools. So, are you going to keep telling me more money will fix this, because I feel like this is much more connected to the problems of people who can't read. Yes, they're going to have problems with gainful employment, and it seems like, you know, a lot of times the solutions that come from the left seem symbolic. They don't seem like we're addressing what really needs to be done, which is get kids learning, get them reading, get them to have a job. It doesn't seem like the money is getting to this problem if 85 percent of Black students lack proficiency in reading skills."

4. February 4, 2023: "If you're part of today's woke revolution you need to study the part of revolutions where they spin out of control because the revolutionaries get so drunk on their own purifying elixir, they imagine they can reinvent the very nature of human beings," Maher said, referencing Chairman Mao's cultural revolution in China from 1966 to 1976. "Those who resisted were attacked by an army of purifiers called the Red Guard, who went around the country putting dunce caps on people who didn't take to being a new kind of mortal being. A lot of pointing and shaming went on, and, oh, about a million dead. And the only way to survive was to plead insanity for the crime of being insufficiently radical and then apologize and thank the state for the chance to see what a piece of shit you are and, of course, submit to re-education, or as we call it in America, freshman orientation."

Boom.

"We do have our own Red Guard here, but they do their rampaging on Twitter."

3. September 3, 2023: "The woke believe race is first and foremost the thing you should always see everywhere, which I find interesting because that used to be the position of the Ku Klux Klan."

2. September 3, 2023: "Liberalism was never 'shoplifting is progressive.' And we weren't interested in legalizing shoplifting, but after the George Floyd murder and riots, there was a movement to disband a lot of the police. . . . And what happened was, of course, crime went up in certain areas, and a lot of the officers who were fired or let go were hired as private security by the rich people, and their neighborhoods stayed safe. That wasn't exactly a victory for Liberalism."

1. March 3, 2021: "We see a problem and we ignore it, lie about it, fight about it, endlessly litigate it, sunset-clause it, kick it down the road, and then write a bill where a half-assed solution doesn't kick in for ten years. China sees a problem and they fix it. They build a dam. We debate what to rename it."

Poignant, hilarious stuff. And if you did an experiment that attributes these comments to Rush Limbaugh instead of Maher, 99.9 percent of those reading or hearing it would fully accept it as fact.

Real Time's guests are also a refreshing mix of perspectives. MSNBC or CNN would be wise to emulate this model, but instead we get a cadre of ex-Obama or Biden officials and Lincoln Projectesque "Republicans" who only get booked to bash Trump in the most provocative and pious ways.

"There may not be a more eclectic guest list on all of television," *Variety* once noted. This is accurate. Because unlike other one-trick-pony programs, Maher can still attract big names from both sides of the aisle, including media figures from the left, right, and center. He could easily ambush conservatives on the program for cheap applause and kudos from cheerleading media reporters. He doesn't. Instead, much like Joe Rogan, he's curious and asks good, tough, but mostly fair questions and keeps things conversational instead of rigid. Most guests don't feel they were used as a prop on Ambush TV as a result.

Rachel Maddow once appeared on *Real Time* in 2012, thinking she was in her usual safe space. But instead she was challenged by another panelist named Nick Gillespie, an unapologetic Libertarian and editor of *Reason* magazine.

The conversation centered on Maddow calling Obamacare a great policy victory for President Obama. So Gillespie asked if she would call Romneycare, Mitt Romney's state-run health care plan, signed into law when he was governor of Massachusetts, a great Republican policy.

"Romneycare is something that you would agree with?" Gillespie said. "You would say that's a great Republican policy?"

"You don't know anything about me!" Maddow, who isn't used to actually ever being challenged on anything throughout her career, bellowed, somehow offended by a perfectly good question. "You should start making your arguments from places other than 'This is something I'm assuming about you.'"

Maher and Gillespie proceeded to press her on the original question: Would you give the same praise to Romney, Obama's presidential opponent that year, that you did to Obama about the same policy?

"Leave me alone about Romneycare!" she shot back before adding this doozy: "Listen, my job is to cover these things, not to tell you how I like them or not."

Rachel Maddow, objective journalist who never attaches her opinion to anything. Check.

She never appeared on *Real Time* again.

Back to Maher: he has heard the criticism from some on the left, calling him a sellout.

"Let's get this straight," he said in an opening monologue in 2022. "It's not me who changed—it's the left, who is now made up of a small contingent who've gone mental, and a large contingent who refuse to call them out for it. But I will."

The monologue was titled "How the Left Was Lost."

There's a reason Maher has survived a quarter century on the air: he keeps things unpredictable and does so from an honest place. You may disagree with his perspective, but at least it's genuine.

And while we're on the topic of being genuine, there's the human antonym in the governor's mansion in California who goes by the name of Gavin Newsom. And he wants to do to America what he's done to California:

Destroy it.

CHAPTER 4

From Slick Willie to Slick Gavin

You have to hand it to California governor Gavin Newsom (D). No other governor in the country can delude themselves so deeply while having such illusions of grandeur. The hunky Democrat absolutely believes he will be president one day. And he'll get to the Oval Office, he thinks, by running on his record in California.

Forget having the highest state income taxes in the country. Forget having the highest poverty rates in the country. Forget rampant drug use and tent cities becoming the norm in San Francisco and Los Angeles. And forget, heading into 2024, a budget shortfall of nearly $35 billion. Yet Newsom thinks he's the best thing to come out of the Golden State since Ronald Reagan.

"Join us in California where we still believe in freedom!" blares a TV ad Newsom ran in Florida. Yup. Yep. The state that kept kids in masks and Covid mandates longer than most in the country is apparently also the state that embraces freedom more than any other. A state that takes more of its citizens' money than any other . . . *that's* the free one when compared to Florida, which takes 0.0 percent of state income tax away from its workers.

In October 2023, Newsom perfectly underscored how utterly and annoyingly woke the party has become by appointing Emily's List president Laphonza Butler to fill a Senate seat left vacant by the death of Dianne Feinstein.

"I have no doubt she will carry the baton left by Senator Feinstein, continue to break glass ceilings, and fight for all Californians in Washington," Newsom declared at the time.

The glass ceilings Newsom is referring to is the fact that Butler can now be called a historic figure because she is the first Black lesbian to serve in the Senate. Were there others far more qualified for the job? Of course. But Newsom chose Butler for the same reason Biden chose Karine Jean-Pierre to be his press secretary. Oh, and here's the best part: Butler is a resident of Maryland and didn't register to vote in California, where she owns property, until *last year*.

As far as Newsom's freedom push, part of that is mandating what kind of car one can purchase.

"We can solve this climate crisis if we focus on the big, bold steps necessary to cut pollution. California now has a groundbreaking, world-leading plan to achieve 100 percent zero-emission vehicle sales by 2035," Newsom announced in 2022.

Looks good on paper. At least until some basic questions are asked. For example, let's say I live in an apartment complex in LA or San Diego. Let's say that the complex has hundreds of units and more than a thousand occupants.

How exactly, Mr. Newsom, am I supposed to charge my vehicle? Will there be hundreds of charging stations in the garage of the unit? What if there is no garage? Oh, and who is supposed to pay for these charging stations? Residents? The landlord? Will the state provide them? If so, who pays for that? And what happens if my charge runs out while sitting in hours of traffic on I-5?

While we're asking questions, how does anyone outside of the upper middle class and rich afford to purchase an electric car? The average cost is currently about $60,000, which means before taxes, I need to earn six figures just to afford to pay for the car with my entire salary for a year. And since there really isn't much of a mass transit system in a city like Los Angeles, I don't have much of an option in terms of getting around.

The overall message is clear: Democrats don't give a crap about the plight of low- and middle-class workers. If they did, they wouldn't ban the sale of cars that they can afford. Note: California's median income per household is $78,000 before taxes. So sure . . . let's have everybody buy an electric car most residents cannot remotely afford.

In a related story, Newsom's own net worth is north of $20 million. *He* can certainly afford it, as can the Pelosis, who are worth more than $100 million. My governor here in Jersey, Phil Murphy, another multimillionaire, also announced this year that he plans to make the state go full electric by 2035. He never explained the whole charging-the-car-in-urban-environments thing either.

In a related story, California and New Jersey are among the worst commuter states in the country. Having lived here most of my life, I can safely say our mass transit system is beyond slow. Example: I live twenty miles from midtown Manhattan, but to get into the city, I need to take one train to Secaucus that includes ten stops along the way (I've seen Jell-O move faster), and then transfer to another train on another floor in that train station to crawl into Manhattan through a perpetually bottlenecked tunnel until the Hudson. And from there, it's fun time on the New York City subway, where crime has skyrocketed and people die from being pushed off platforms all too often.

All told, this hellscape of a commute takes more than *ninety minutes to go twenty miles*. But Murphy could not care less. The guy owns an opulent villa in Italy that includes a horse stable and tennis court that he jetted off to at the height of Covid. And when he is here, he doesn't drive anywhere himself.

What these elitist leaders don't get is that people are generally smart when it comes to this stuff. Murphy was nearly voted out in 2021 in a state he won by 14 points four years prior, while Newsom was nearly recalled in 2021 after winning by 24 points in 2018.

The GOP may have only generated a red ripple instead of a red wave in the 2022 midterms, but a red tsunami is continuing in 2023 for the foreseeable future: the mass exodus out of blue states to red states.

Recent US Census data underscore an alarming reality for California, New York, and Illinois . . . more people are moving out than moving in.

The exodus is very real: California lost nearly 350,000 residents in 2022, while New York lost about 300,000 and Illinois saw more than 140,000 go elsewhere, per census numbers. Other states, including New Jersey (–64,231), Massachusetts (–57,292), and Pennsylvania (–39,957), also saw large numbers of residents getting out.

Meanwhile other states, such as Florida and Texas, saw large gains in population, with Florida adding an eye-popping 444,484 residents and Texas adding 470,708. Other population winners include North Carolina (99,796 residents added), South Carolina (+84,030), Tennessee (+81,646), and Georgia (+81,406).

Not coincidentally, all these southern states except North Carolina have Republican governors, while California, New York, Illinois, New Jersey, Massachusetts, and Pennsylvania have Democratic governors.

U-Haul, America's largest moving company, recently released data underscoring the census figures. California, the state with the most electoral votes (55), ranked *last* in terms of migration numbers. Illinois ranked 49th, just ahead of Michigan, Massachusetts, New York, and New Jersey.

In most of these states, the recipe for the exodus has three primary ingredients:

Taxes. Traffic. Crime.

On the third front, things are so bad in progressive San Francisco that it fired its district attorney last year. New York saw a record 4,500-plus police officers resign as violent crime rose 22 percent from the year before. And Mayor Lori Lightfoot lost her reelection bid in Chicago, with just 9 percent of voters saying that the city was headed in the right direction, according to a poll from the *Chicago Index*.[*] Crime is the major reason why.

The post–COVID-19 world compelled many employers to embrace a work-from-anywhere model. Given how horrific commutes into and out of those cities can be, getting dozens of hours of time back every week makes workers happier and more productive. So if most employees want to leave New York or Chicago or Los Angeles for Tampa or Austin or Nashville, they may be able to do so without leaving their jobs, thereby fueling the exodus.

These migration patterns have had huge consequences for state budgets, per the Internal Revenue Service. New York's tax base, for example, decreased by $19.5 billion in 2020, while California saw $17.8 billion leave that year. Illinois lost $8.5 billion. Meanwhile, Florida *gained* $23.7 billion in gross income, while Texas saw $6.3 billion added to its state coffers. Other states also all saw positive gains in tax revenue: North Carolina ($3.8 billion), South Carolina ($3.6 billion), and Tennessee ($2.6 billion).

There are political ramifications to consider as well. The most recent census resulted in Republicans gaining House seats. In a razor-thin majority, these extra seats were crucial in handing the GOP the majority. The wealth of tax revenue coming from an influx of new residents has helped red state governors such as Ron DeSantis. Meanwhile, in New York, Democratic governor Kathy Hochul proposed a $227 billion budget for fiscal year 2024. Compare that number to Florida's proposed budget, which comes in at $115 billion.

Why the comparison to New York? Because Florida has a larger population (21.78 million) than the Empire State (19.84 million), yet it spends *half* as much money to run the state. "This is just people voting

---

* Greg Hinz, "Chicagoans in a Sour Mood as Elections for Mayor, Governor Near," *Crain's Chicago Business*, January 13, 2022, https://www.chicagobusiness.com /chicago-index/chicago-index-survey-signals-locals-fear-crime-spike-worry-about -city-direction.

with their feet," DeSantis once observed. And he's right. And it's not just residents leaving, either. The pace of businesses leaving California, for example, more than doubled in 2021 compared to 2020, according to a recent report from Stanford University.

The report shows that more than 150 companies moved their respective headquarters last year, compared to just 75 the previous year. More context: just 46 companies departed in 2018.

More notable of these departures is Elon Musk's Tesla, which grabbed major headlines after the vocal CEO announced he was relocating his electric car headquarters from Silicon Valley to Austin, Texas. Musk pointed to affordable housing and shorter commute times as key factors. And crime is also a factor, as cited by billionaire hedge fund boss Ken Griffin, who moved his firm Citadel from Chicago to Miami.

"If people aren't safe here, they're not going to live here," Griffin explained when announcing the move. "I've had multiple colleagues mugged at gunpoint. I've had a colleague stabbed on the way to work. Countless issues of burglary. I mean, that's a really difficult backdrop" to draw talent to places like Chicago.

So if a future presidential race ends up being DeSantis versus, say, California governor Gavin Newsom in 2028, Americans will be given a simple contrast and choice: Which state do you want the country to resemble most, Florida or California?

That's not a difficult choice, is it?

Another not-so-difficult choice was deciding who would replace Circle Back Jen Psaki as White House press secretary in 2022 after she ran to MSNBC. At the bottom of the list, next to Baghdad Bob, should have been Karine Jean-Pierre, formerly of (drumroll) MSNBC. But the Biden White House is all about checking off boxes . . . basic ability to do the job be damned.

CHAPTER 5

Baghdad Jean-Pierre

When thinking of White House press secretary Karine Jean-Pierre, only one word comes to mind:

Amateur.

And this perspective comes from someone who has said many times in the past that one of the most difficult white-collar jobs in the world is to be the president's spokesperson. We saw it with Jean-Pierre's predecessor in the pious Jen Psaki; the job calls for defending the indefensible. And when an overwhelming number of voters believed (and still believe) that the country is headed in the wrong direction, as they did throughout 2022, when Jean-Pierre took the job, and when the president has polled in the 20s and 30s on approval in terms of his handling of the border or inflation, that's not a job most would sign up for.[*]

But Jean-Pierre isn't just a victim of bad luck and timing. This is a press secretary who oftentimes reads scripted answers from a binder the size of Foggy Bottom . . . *verbatim.* She is so dependent on the binder that she has actually read the wrong answers to questions.

Check out this exchange between the press secretary and Peter Doocy

---

* Darragh Roche, "Joe Biden's Approval Rating Falls to Near Record Low amid Inflation Fears," *Newsweek*, May 10, 2022, https://www.newsweek.com/joe-biden-approval-rating-falls-near-record-low-inflation-fears-1705078.

when, after Biden argued that taxing corporations will somehow bring down inflation ("You want to bring down inflation? Let's make sure the wealthiest corporations pay their fair share," the president, or whoever writes his stuff, strangely tweeted in 2022), Doocy asked Jean-Pierre about high inflation. What followed was like listening to a sophomore putting together a series of sentences in order to achieve a mandatory word count on a term paper.

Here it is verbatim, per the official White House transcript. Read it several times, and you'll have zero idea what Jean-Pierre is talking about. And again, this is the *White House friggin' press secretary.*

Doocy: *"How does raising taxes on corporations lower the cost of gas, the cost of a used car, the cost of food, for everyday Americans?"*

Jean-Pierre: *"So, look, I think we encourage those who have done very well—right?—especially those who care about climate change, to support a fairer tax—tax code that doesn't change—that doesn't charge manufacturers' workers, cops, builders a higher percentage of their earnings; that the most fortunate people in our nation—and not let the—that stand in the way of reducing energy costs and fighting this existential problem, if you think about that as an example, and to support basic collective bargaining rights as well. Right? That's also important. But look, it is—you know, by not—if—without having a fairer tax code, which is what I'm talking about, then all—every—like manufacturing workers, cops—you know, it's not fair for them to have to pay higher taxes than the folks that—who are—who are—who are not paying taxes at all or barely have."*

Again, the original question was about how raising taxes on corporations lowers inflation. Where, in that Thousand Island word salad, is *any* of that addressed? And if corporations are paying "more of their fair share," you'll never guess who those corporations will pass that cost on to:

a) You
b) Me
c) Your neighbors
d) Consumers in general
e) All of the above

Jen Psaki had plenty of flaws, for sure, the biggest of them being so utterly condescending while being blatantly dishonest. Psaki's greatest hits include pushing hilariously false narratives such as blaming Donald Trump for the current border crisis, arguing that spending additional trillions will lower inflation and the deficit, and claiming that Republicans want to defund the police. But Psaki at least had a sense of confidence behind her answers, whether they were truthful or not. Psaki eventually and predictably moved on to MSNBC, leading to Jean-Pierre's promotion.

Then, of course, there's the question of Jean-Pierre's credibility based on her past statements that, if uttered by a conservative or anyone named Trump, would be characterized as a "chilling attack on democracy."

"Stolen election . . . welcome to the world of #unpresidented Trump," she tweeted after the 2016 election.

"Trump always finds a way to take it to the lowest of lows. Not only is he a petulant dotard but also a deplorable illegitimate president" was her sentiment in 2017.

"Reminder: Brian Kemp stole the gubernatorial election from Georgians and Stacey Abrams," she said of Abrams's gubernatorial loss to Republican Brian Kemp in 2018.

Twitter, in the pre–Elon Musk era, did not suspend Jean-Pierre's account, nor did it take those tweets down, even though they broke the platform's number one rule regarding false or misleading claims. Musk was 100 percent correct: the platform had a "very far-left bias."

Jean-Pierre should apologize, but that ain't happening and absolutely never will because her allies in the media, and there are many, ain't broaching them or calling her a conspiracy theorist. Picture the same treatment of Kayleigh McEnany, win valuable prizes.

When Jean-Pierre first took the job in 2022, allies in the press didn't scrutinize her past reckless statements, but instead made the focus (ding ding ding!) her gender and color and sexual orientation.

Karine Jean-Pierre leads history-making first briefing as White House press secretary.

—*USA TODAY*

New press secretary hails barrier breakers who paved the way for her.
—*NBC NEWS*

Biden's press secretary Karine Jean-Pierre poses in White House dress designed by Ivanka Trump.

—*DAILY MAIL*

If Jean-Pierre is wise, she would reach out to past successful press secretaries who served under Democratic presidents. Mike McCurry was excellent under Bill Clinton, as was Robert Gibbs under President Obama. You can disagree with the message, but those guys knew how to communicate, and did so with the kind of gravitas this position used to have. It's a smart bet that all of these former press secretaries would be happy to help, but don't expect that to happen.

John Kirby, the former Pentagon spokesperson, absolutely should have this job based on merit and based on the fact that he's also good at what he does . . . but he was passed over for other reasons that included not checking off the right boxes for some cheap headlines.

Instead, the press is fed this nonsense on a daily basis.

"Is the administration trying to protect the president from our questions? Please answer that question," reporter Jon Decker once asked Jean-Pierre.

"Absolutely not. Absolutely not," she replied.

"Then why the lack of any interaction in a formal setting to have a press conference?" Decker followed.

After some back-and-forth, Jean-Pierre landed on this non-answer:

"The President many times has stood in front of all of you, has taken questions on his own, because he wanted to see what was on—on your minds, he wanted to see what the questions you all were going to ask him, and he wanted to answer them directly," she claimed before eventually adding, "I'll say this: It is also unprecedented that a President takes as many shouted questions as this President has. And he has."

That's simply beyond false to the point of insulting. As we've seen time and again, Biden morphs into Christian McCaffrey right after making a statement or speech by practically running off the stage with sudden speed and agility as reporters are shouting questions. When reporters are invited into the Oval Office, they're screamed out of the room by the president's handlers when it's normally Q&A time. And most of the press corps just takes it.

For context in the modern era, George H. W. Bush had ninety solo press conferences in his first and only term. Bill Clinton had fifty-nine over two terms. George W. Bush had forty-nine over his eight years. Barack Obama had sixty-four from 2009 to 2016. Donald Trump had forty-four from 2017 to 2021, but on dozens of occasions held gaggles (unofficial press conferences) with reporters outside of the White House on his way to Marine One.

But Joe Biden? He held zero solo press conferences on US soil in 2023. ZERO. We've gone from the most accessible president of our lifetimes in Trump to the most protected and packaged. Karine Jean-Pierre knows this, of course, but lies anyway because the fact-checkers won't dare fact-check her. For proof, just go to PolitiFact and do a search under Jean-Pierre's name. In 2023 she wasn't fact-checked for saying insane things like that the Biden administration has inherited the border crisis from Trump. Overall in 2022 and 2023, Jean-Pierre has been fact-checked a grand total of *four times*.

It wasn't always this way. Another Pierre, Pierre Salinger, served as press secretary for Presidents John F. Kennedy and Lyndon B. Johnson back in the 1960s. He later served in the Senate. Salinger would later go on to work for ABC Sports before moving to the news division, and won the prestigious George Polk Award in 1981 for his scoop on the United States holding secret talks with Iran to free American hostages being held in Tehran. He would go on to write six books.

Mike McCurry is another Democratic White House press secretary I came to admire. The guy simply came across as credible, and we never saw the Acosta-like drama between reporters and McCurry during the press briefings, which McCurry had decided to have televised for the first time starting in 1995 in an effort toward maximum transparency and access.

When McCurry stepped down in 1998, here was the *Washington Post* review of his tenure via Peter Baker and Howard Kurtz: "McCurry, 43, valued his reputation for honesty, which remained largely intact. For all of the adversarial moments, he managed the near-impossible by staying popular with both colleagues and reporters," they wrote. "McCurry became the most recognizable face on the Clinton White House staff with televised daily briefings flavored by detailed explanations of policy and punctuated by pithy one-liners intended to defuse tense moments. Credited with repairing frayed relations with the news media, he was on the front lines for Clinton on nearly every major battle from budget wars to campaign finance improprieties."

Could anyone see Jean-Pierre having the same post–White House life as Salinger or receiving that kind of review from the *Post*? Nope. She'll probably be added to the cast of *The View* instead, a liberal bastion that also loves to check off boxes and a place where stupidity is not a handicap.

Speaking of checking off boxes, let's move on to the ultimate example of a DEI hire: Peter Paul Montgomery Buttigieg, transportation aficionado. . . .

PART II

Remember When Democrats Cared about the Working Class?

"Today, the average gas price in America hit an all-time record high of over $4 per gallon. Okay, that stings, but a clear conscience is worth a buck or two. I'm willing to pay. I'm willing to pay $4 a gallon. Hell, I'll pay $15 a gallon because I drive a Tesla."

That's Democratic activist and multimillionaire "comedian" Stephen Colbert defending high gas prices under Joe Biden because, unlike most people, he can actually afford a Tesla.

If the definition of the word *elitist* needs a poster boy, it's Colbert. The sanctimonious host speaks down about Trump and his supporters on a nightly basis while welcoming fellow millionaires like Senator Bernie Sanders on his program.

Carson had Rickles. Letterman had Regis. Colbert has . . . Bernie. And on one occasion, he asked the Democratic socialist about his private jet use, but not in the way such a climate-conscious host would normally take on a hypocritical climate-destroying Republican senator.

"Are you going to give rides to the other candidates who are in the Senate?" Colbert asked.

"Actually, we have used jets previously, and that was an idea we thought of. Those are expensive so we thought we'd all chip in and ride together," Sanders said.

"That's greener. That's greener, sir," the insufferable host replied.

Overall, Bernie has spent boatloads of money to fly private, as did Joe Biden and Elizabeth Warren and John Kelly, who all championed the Green New Deal. But remember, they will insist, Democrats are the party of the workingman and -woman.

Overall, per IRS figures, about two-thirds (65 percent) of the US households that earn more than $500,000 per year are in Democratic districts, while 74 percent of households in GOP districts earn less than $100,000 per year. Throw in the fact that the ten richest congressional districts in the United States have representatives in Congress with a (D) next to their names, and this is what the Blue Team has become: The party that's all about green . . . green energy except when needing to get from point A to point B in luxury . . . and green as in raking in cash from the same richest 1 percent they used to rail against.

They are the champagne socialists. And the irony to end all ironies is this: the man they see as the biggest threat to the country and the planet, Donald Trump, is the billionaire who is connecting with blue-collar voters and working-class people. Why? Because he doesn't piously tell them how to think or feel. He connects. He's tough like them. He won't be pushed around. He's imperfect. And he actually has this thing called a sense of humor.

Authenticity cannot be taught, a prominent TV executive once told me. Warts and all, that's crucial in politics today, given the exposure we have to these people through 24/7 cable news and 24/7 social media. And most Democrats simply seem to be performance artists and nothing else, including the focus of our next chapter, who looks and sounds like he was created as a cyborg in a woke lab. . . .

CHAPTER 6

Meet Elite Pete, Your Future President

The year is 2023. The month is February. It is now more than two years since the Trump administration left town. And during those two years, the Democratic Party controlled the House, the Senate, and the Oval Office. Yet, as we have seen time and time and time again, Team Biden refuses to take any responsibility for the hot mess in a dumpster fire they have created.

Exhibit A is the train derailment that occurred in East Palestine, Ohio, on February 3 of that year. The Norfolk Southern train was carrying a toxin called vinyl chloride, along with three other cancer-causing chemicals. Hazmat crews conducted a controlled burn of those toxic chemicals, sending them into the air and water. Fish and poultry were found dead shortly thereafter. And residents in East Palestine and the surrounding areas began reporting bouts of headaches, dizziness, nausea, and respiratory issues.

East Palestine is a lower-middle-class working town. When you think of the Rust Belt, East Palestine is as exemplary as it gets. Its median household income is just below $45,000 per year (the national average is $70,000). Hundreds of residents live below the poverty level.

We've talked about the Democratic Party no longer being a champion for the little guy in towns like East Palestine, but one that caters to the elites. And when you think of what an elitist looks and sounds like, look no further than Transportation Secretary Pete Buttigieg.

The media darling has been called "the future of the Democratic Party." They say he's super smart, too. It must be pretty great to be the smartest man in the swamp!

The former mayor of relatively tiny South Bend, Indiana, was nominated to be Joe Biden's transportation secretary—presumably as a thank-you for dropping out of the 2020 presidential race in early March despite beating Biden in Iowa and New Hampshire. It was seemingly the plan all along: clear a path for the old man and make voters believe they would be getting a moderate, a uniter, a swell guy, as the Democratic alternative to the evil Donald Trump.

Of course, Biden could have nominated Buttigieg for some meaningless job in his box-checking diversity hire exercise. Perhaps ambassador to Portugal, or assistant to the traveling Climate Czar, John Kerry. Both men love flying private, after all. But for reasons that defy logic, Buttigieg was nominated to run the sprawling Transportation Department, which has about sixty thousand employees and a budget north of $200 billion.

South Bend is home to the University of Notre Dame. It has a bus station with a relatively small fleet of buses, a small train station, and a small regional airport. So, who better for Biden to nominate as secretary of the DOT? Was Hunter Biden not available?

In his first year on the job, as a supply chain crisis was exploding in ports from Los Angeles to Charleston, Buttigieg decided to take some time off after he and his husband successfully adopted twin babies. And just how long was this paternity leave for this senior cabinet member?

Try *two months*.

Of course, being an elitist means doing whatever you want, whenever you want. In Pete's case, he simply decided to take off without, you know, letting the public know. Per *Politico*'s Playbook newsletter in October 2021:

"They didn't previously announce it, but Buttigieg's office told West Wing Playbook that the secretary has actually been on paid leave since mid-August to spend time with his husband, Chasten, and their two newborn babies."

So some obvious questions here: Why wasn't an acting secretary named while Secretary Buttigieg was on paternity leave for two months? Why didn't the White House or Buttigieg himself announce he was going to be out for nearly nine weeks starting in August? Nothing was revealed until *Politico* contacted Buttigieg's office.

Pete would not even visit a port to assess the blockages and delays surrounding a supply chain crisis until six months after the crisis began. Woody Allen once famously said that 90 percent of success is showing up. The former mayor failed to do that time and time and time again.

Things only got worse when the commercial airline industry collapsed over the Christmas holidays in 2022. A few months earlier, in the summer of 2022, Buttigieg kept assuring us things would improve. But on Christmas morning, while Pete was celebrating the holiday at his home in Michigan, millions of travelers were stranded for days, with thousands spending Christmas Eve sleeping on the floors of airports across the country.

Just a few weeks later, the East Palestine disaster happened. And for ten days Buttigieg said absolutely nothing about it, despite residents getting sick while seeing their property values plummet. During any catastrophe, leaders must get out of their offices and off their asses and travel to a disaster site under their purview to assess damage, weigh what resources can be utilized, and show solidarity with the folks who are impacted. Buttigieg did no such thing. It's a head-in-the-sand approach that had many Ohio residents angry.

"Where's Pete Buttigieg? Where's he at?" one resident asked East Palestine mayor Trent Conaway.

"I don't know. Your guess is as good as [mine]," Conaway replied.

As the media finally descended on East Palestine and the complaints rightly got louder, Buttigieg was suddenly on the defensive. Did he accept any accountability? Of course not. Instead, he resorted to blaming (you guessed it) Trump for what was happening in Ohio.

"We're constrained by law on some areas of rail regulation (like the braking rule withdrawn by the Trump administration in 2018 because of a law passed by Congress in 2015), but we are using the powers we do have to keep people safe," Buttigieg tweeted. "And of course, I'm always ready to work with Congress on furthering (or in some cases, restoring) our capacity to address rail safety issues."

So, despite Democrats having controlled the House, Senate, and White House for two years, Buttigieg claimed his hands were tied because of an administration that departed in January 2021. And of course our stenography media went with the desired narrative. Because Trump.

Politico: *"Trump's Visit to Ohio Derailment Gives Biden's Team Some Breathing Room: His Planned Appearance near the Scene of This Month's Toxic Derailment Has Democrats Pointing to His Past Efforts to Roll Back Train and Chemical Regulations"*

USA Today: *"White House Blames Trump Administration and Republicans over East Palestine, Ohio, Spill"*

And again, instead of Pete going to Ohio or meeting with the head of Norfolk Southern and demanding accountability, here's what we got instead:

ABC News: *"Ohio Train Derailment: Buttigieg Pens Sharply Worded Letter to Norfolk Southern Railway"*

This laughable and limp response is reminiscent of Leonardo DiCaprio's Jack Dawson character during the floating-door scene with Kate Winslet's Rose DeWitt Bukater in 1997's *Titanic*. Jack is suffering from hypothermia after allowing Rose to stay on the door while he is forced to stay in the freezing water, but he still has a sense of humor regarding the unsinkable ship actually sinking.

"I don't know about you, but I intend on writing a strongly worded letter to the White Star Line about all of this," a shivering Jack on the verge of death muses. So that's what Buttigieg did: write a strongly worded letter to the train company. That'll totally work.

Only after former president Trump visited East Palestine to hand out supplies and speak with local residents did Buttigieg finally find the time to visit the town . . . nearly three weeks after the derailment. And just like that, the usual suspects in the press did everything they could to protect Biden and Buttigieg.

Vox: *"Ohio Train Derailment: Why Republicans Seized on the East Palestine Accident"*

Rolling Stone: *"Trump Bashes Biden Then Jets to McDonald's during East Palestine Visit"*

NBC News: *"With Visit to East Palestine, Trump Picks a Fight He Can't Win"*

CNN: *"Ohio's Toxic Spill Is Unleashing Poisonous, Partisan Politics"*

You gotta love the framing of the CNN piece. By the way, here's a dirty little trick that outlets like CNN or the *Washington Post* always try to pull: publish an opinion piece from a proven partisan whose title is "White House reporter" and call the opinion another name to throw off the scent:

"Analysis."

This particular op-ed, er . . . analysis was written by Stephen Collinson, who has doled out these kinds of gems while covering President Biden:

CNN.com: *"President Biden to Showcase His Moderate Radicalism in His Big Congressional Address"*

Moderate radicalism. Is that an oxymoron, like *jumbo shrimp*? A working vacation?

"Biden's quiet radicalism is expressed through a huge pandemic rescue bill, a larger proposal that redefines the concept of infrastructure, and a massive health and child care blueprint," wrote Collinson, who could have simply used some word economy and called these proposals a socialist blueprint.

As you may have guessed, Pete Buttigieg wants to be president one day. His fellow elites in the media think he's da bomb, but the rest of the country, outside the blind partisans, loathes anyone who looks down at them. It's why Hillary lost after her "deplorables" comment. It's why a cackling Kamala, who gives speeches in the same tone that I use when trying to teach my second grader about the solar system, is so unpopular. It's why John Kerry and Al Gore have been reduced to punch lines on climate while doing some of the worst things an individual can do to destroy it.

"To me, it's his job. And this is something that he should be here for. This is pretty significant," East Palestine resident Linda Murphy told *Fox & Friends* two weeks after the accident. "The amount of chemicals, cancer-causing chemicals that were released and what we're left to deal with. We need a little bit of guidance here. And I don't know, I think that this deserves a pink slip for his job."

Don't expect that to happen. This is a president who seems unwilling to fire anybody despite their failing grades. And with the media largely cheering him, Pete will still be the Democratic nominee one day. He checks off all the right boxes, and journalists who are supposed to speak truth to power will make excuses for his horrific tenure as transportation secretary. You can bookmark that.

Something else that can be taken to the bank is the fact that there are *far* more perks to being a Democrat than a Republican. Allow me to count the ways. . . .

CHAPTER 7

It Really Is Good to Be a Democrat

If considering getting into politics, and survival along with the basic comfort of not being challenged by the press in any capacity is the goal, which party would you decide to join if you had no true principles to guide your ideology?

a) Republican
b) Democrat

If you answered b, put on that Captain Obvious hat and pat yourself on the back. Because if you're a Republican, you're already ten laps behind your opponent based on the rules of the game. There's also a very strong chance you'll be painted a racist. You'll also be accused of being anti-LGBTQ. And don't forget about being a member of the party of election deniers (Hillary Clinton? Stacey Abrams? Naah . . . they don't count on this front). And finally, you'll be accused of knowingly wanting to destroy the planet because you don't support spending trillions to battle the Climate Crisis.

For a prime example of this advantage in modern politics, I give one name:

John Karl Fetterman.

The onetime lieutenant governor of Pennsylvania is a different kind of politician. He's a towering and bald fiftysomething man-child. He rarely wears suits or even a sports coat, instead opting for hoodies and shorts while sporting a goatee, as if he's heading to your average beer pong tournament.

As you know, Fetterman suffered a massive stroke in May 2022. At the time, he had already announced his run for Pennsylvania's open Senate seat after Republican Pat Toomey announced his retirement. And for months after his stroke, he was absent from the campaign trail.

Fetterman's campaign said he had trouble with auditory processing. And during the times he would do a rare T-ball interview with outlets like MSNBC, he needed a teleprompter to read the questions as a result. His opponent, the Trump-endorsed Dr. Mehmet Oz, offered to debate Fetterman five times, including before early voting began in the state on September 19. Local affiliates offered to broadcast the interviews. But Fetterman declined all but one debate, which took place just days before the election and after hundreds of thousands of votes were cast.

"As I recover from this stroke and improve my auditory processing and speech, I look forward to continuing to meet with the people of Pennsylvania," Fetterman said in a statement after the Oz campaign offered to debate in September. "They'll always know where I stand."

For Democrats, the Pennsylvania race was seen as crucial, given the Senate was fifty-fifty at the time. But it was obvious Fetterman was in no condition to be in the race, let alone the US Senate. If *anyone* had any integrity or actually cared about the man, they would have had the balls to respectfully suggest that he should back out of the race and take time to recover.

Note: One quarter of stroke victims go on to have a second stroke. But Democrats only cheered Fetterman on, led by Joe Biden and Mrs. Fetterman and most pathetically by the media, who all campaigned vigorously for him despite fully knowing the risk. The candidate also refused to release his medical records, an obvious sign that all was not well. And during his campaign stops in the fall, he often stumbled rhetorically, and his sentences were frequently disjointed. Here's a transcript from a rally in Pittsburgh from September 2022, for example:

"Send me to Washington, D.C., to send—so I can work with Senator Casey. And I can champion the union way of life—in Jersey, excuse me, in D.C. Thank you. Thank you very much. And it's an honor—I live eight minutes away from here. And when I leave tonight, I got, three miles away, Dr. Oz in his mansion in New Jersey. You've got a friend and you have an ally. Send me to Washington, D.C. Thank you very much."

If this was a professional boxing match, the ref would have declared a TKO right at that moment. As for the press, outside of the *Pittsburgh Post-Gazette* and *Washington Post*, no entity, including the *New York Times* and Pennsylvania's largest newspaper, the *Philadelphia Inquirer*, called on Fetterman to release his medical records.

"Fetterman 2022: The Steampunk Version of Biden in His Basement," read one *New York Times* headline instead.

"As he recovers from a stroke, the Democratic Senate nominee in Pennsylvania is running a virtual campaign of online memes and withering mockery of his opponent, Dr. Mehmet Oz," this nonopinion "news story" continued. "More than a month into his recovery, Fetterman is trying something utterly novel in American politics: a towel-snapping virtual campaign of sassy online memes, withering mockery of his opponent, Dr. Mehmet Oz, and fourth-wall-bending television ads and online videos that explode many of the usual tropes of political campaigns," it later added, with everything but the pom-poms. Funny how a Trump meme can be seen as mean-spirited and beneath the office, while Fetterman's campaign does the same thing and it's celebrated.

Just one more reason why it's good to be a Democrat.

As Election Day drew closer, in one of the rare instances an actual reporter got access to Fetterman, the report wasn't good. Per NBC's Dasha Burns:

"Because of his stroke, Fetterman's campaign required closed captioning technology for this interview to essentially read our questions as we asked them. And . . . in small talk before the interview without captioning, it wasn't clear he was understanding our conversation," she reported on October 11.

Burns was promptly eviscerated for simply telling the truth.

Associated Press: *"NBC Reporter's Comment about Fetterman Draws Criticism"*

Mediaite: *"Stroke-Survivor Journo Leads Backlash against NBC's Dasha Burns Reporting on Computer-Aided Fetterman Interview"*

The Independent: *"Kara Swisher Shuts Down 'Nonsense' Claims That John Fetterman Couldn't Follow Conversation"*

When it finally came time to debate, Fetterman's cognitive and rhetorical difficulties came on full display for the nation to see. And it was painful to watch and listen to right out of the gate.

"Hi! Good night, everybody!" Those marked Fetterman's first four words of the evening.

It would get worse from there when the moderators, who were excellent that night in asking fair and pointed questions about major issues because they were local reporters and not diva TV hosts, asked him to square his comments about fracking, which he was against before he was for it.

Fetterman in September 2016: "I am not pro-fracking and have stated that if we did things right in this state, we wouldn't have fracking. The industry is a stain on our state and natural resources."

Fetterman right before the election: "I do support fracking, and I don't, I don't—I support fracking, and I stand, and I do support fracking."

By the way, it is amusing to look at stories from the Obama era and compare them to today regarding the issue of fracking.

The *Washington Post* editorial board (when Obama was president): "There's No Need to Panic over Fracking-Related Quakes."

"The goal must be to fully account for fracking's risks to the ambient environment and the atmosphere in regulation, then let the country reap the economic and environmental benefits of low-cost and cleaner-burning natural gas," the board wrote in March 2015.

The *Washington Post* editorial board (when Trump was president): "Trump Is Tearing Up Fracking Rules on FEDERAL LANDS. BE ALARMED."

"The Trump administration announced late last month that it was tearing up rules on hydraulic fracturing—better known as fracking—on federal lands. The change satisfies drillers who have long opposed federal regulations on the controversial oil and gas extraction process. But it should alarm everyone else," they warned in 2018.

Fracking.

Obama.

Good.

Fracking.

Trump.

Bad.

Anyway, getting back to Fetterman and that October 2022 debate, it was called a disaster by almost everyone, and many (including me) thought the race would turn for Oz. But the endorsements came flying in anyway, from everyone from Oprah to the *Philadelphia Inquirer*.

"An experienced public servant, Fetterman has an abundance of the kind of values and priorities that are needed to move the nation forward—and to earn this board's support. The *Inquirer* endorses John Fetterman for U.S. Senate," the *Philadelphia Inquirer* board said in its endorsement shortly before the election.

When we talk about journalism morphing into activism, this is Exhibit A. Control of the Senate was at stake, after all.

By the way, here's the same *Inquirer* hyperventilating over the health of Donald Trump—who at last check never suffered a stroke—after

Trump made a (gasp) visit to Walter Reed Medical Center in November 2019: "Trump's Health under Scrutiny Again after Unplanned Visit to Medical Center"; "Trump Stayed Out of the Public Eye Monday amid Renewed Questions about the Status of His Health and the White House's Handling of his Medical Information."

And then there was that time when Trump, in dress shoes following a commencement speech at West Point, walked cautiously down a wet ramp at the academy. He didn't fall, didn't even stumble, but walking slowly was a big no-no for the Brady Bunch panels on CNN and MSNBC and in the pages of the *Post* and *Times*:

New York Times: *"Trump's Halting Walk down Ramp Raises New Health Questions"*

MSNBC: *"Unsteady Appearance Prompts New Scrutiny of Trump's Health"*

CNN: *"Why the Donald Trump–West Point Ramp Story Actually Matters"*

Washington Post: *"'Like a Baby Deer on a Frozen Pond': Late-Night Hosts Mock Trump over 'Ramp-Gate'"*

This book really does write itself sometimes.

Fetterman would go on to win his race against Oz by a comfortable margin of five points. As it did for Biden, the basement strategy worked again. And we can expect to see that more from Democrats moving forward: avoid anything remotely resembling a tough interview. Say as little as possible. Avoid debating unless absolutely necessary. Lie with impunity, because many in the media will allow it, given which party and opponent is the target.

But in February 2023, not long after Fetterman was sworn in, he was back in the hospital for what his office called "lightheadedness." He remained under observation for days. And not long after that, he was admitted to Walter Reed for what he claimed to be clinical depression, and would remain there for six weeks.

Did anyone in the press witness this and come forward to say that maybe, *just maybe*, it was wrong to endorse this guy so vigorously? Did anyone later say that they should have been steadfast in insisting he release his medical records? Of course not. Instead, these morons, and that's being generous, *even after* he was released from Walter Reed, having been there for most of his time "serving" as a US senator, took things to a profoundly batshit-crazy level.

"Your trajectory from mayor to lieutenant governor, United States senator, was still pointing up. At 53 in politics, that's a young man. Can you have aspirations? Can you serve beyond the United States Senate?" asked a giddy Jane Pauley on CBS after Fetterman was released.

Gisele Fetterman, who was sitting by her husband during the interview, seemed intrigued by the question. For his part, Fetterman said his aspiration for now was to serve in the Senate, but he didn't rule out the President Fetterman possibility.

Can you believe this? Fetterman spends a majority of his first few months in the Senate in a psych ward, and an anchor on a major national news network is asking him about pursuing the presidency? Pauley must have received her cue from MSNBC's Katy Tur, who said after Fetterman's victory that she could see "Fetterman as a [Democratic] nominee at some point for president."

This is utter madness. There should be calls for him to resign from office for the good of his health and safety, especially considering he has a family that includes three children to consider. But nope: there are some who actually believe John Fetterman can run the country one day. And of course, these are the very same people who look the other way when Joe Biden is on vacation for 40 percent of his presidency.

In September 2023, Fetterman once again got treatment only a Democrat could receive. Because it was then that Senate Majority Leader Chuck Schumer decided to loosen a long-standing rule that senators must show up for work in a suit. The rule change was to appease Fetterman, because asking this petulant person to dress like an adult is apparently too much.

Fetterman's choice in fashion isn't surprising, however. This is a guy who lived off his parents into his forties and has never held any job outside politics in his life. *Entitled* is the only word that comes to mind.

"I do not look like a typical politician, nor do I look like a typical person," Fetterman wrote in a Medium blog post in 2021. "I even lack the political metaphorical sleeves to roll up—all I ever wear are short-sleeve work shirts because hard work is the only way to build our communities back up."

Oh, please. You're just lazy and immature.

"I don't mean to look scary, it's just kind of what I have to work with. Maybe that's why my tattoos are *literally* the first thing people Google about me." He proceeded to dedicate four paragraphs in this vapid post to his various tattoos and the meaning behind them.

So did Schumer's new rule apply to Senate staffers who earn far less than the $174,000 Fetterman is paid annually? Can they also show up in shorts and hoodies whenever *they* please? Of course not. They are all still mandated to wear suits—because somehow the new relaxed rule only applies to those who should be leading by example. "Suits for thee, not for me" could be Fetterman's next campaign bumper sticker.

Fortunately, the rule was reversed after some Democratic senators privately complained. But Fetterman got what he wanted by somehow being portrayed as a sympathetic figure in the press.

"If those jagoffs in the House stop trying to shut our government down," Fetterman posted on X, "and fully support Ukraine, then I will save democracy by wearing a suit on the Senate floor next week."

Yes, jagoffs. Take a bow, 51.2 percent of Pennsylvania. This is your freshman senator and possibly your future president.

It really is good to be a Democrat.

Arizona secretary of state Katie Hobbs is now the governor of Arizona thanks to this strategy. She almost entirely avoided the media and rejected the opportunity to debate her opponent, Republican Kari Lake.

"It's clear that Kari Lake is much more interested in creating a spectacle and having the spotlight than actually having a substantive discussion about the issues," Hobbs told Chuck Todd during a T-ball session on NBC's *Meet the Press*. The moderator offered almost no pushback and instead proposed a Lincoln-Douglas debate without a moderator. Hobbs responded by repeating herself, saying she was open to having a "substantive discussion" with Lake. It never happened, and there was little pressure from the press to do so.

One of the best nonpartisan journalists in the game today is Jonathan Swan, my former colleague at *The Hill*. Here's what he once tweeted regarding his efforts to land a one-on-one interview with President Biden:

"I say this as somebody who has tried repeatedly to get a one-on-one with Joe Biden. He won't do it. And there's no convening power on planet earth that could compel him to do an interview that his advisers deem to be unsafe. This is of course true of many politicians."

And Swan's 100 percent correct. Biden did a total of seven solo press conferences in 2022. For context, Trump did *thirty-five* during his final year in office.

But remember, Trump was bad for the free press despite being the most accessible president in history, according to all the media members who got rich off of their so-called tell-all books about the forty-fifth president. Biden turns and runs after almost every public appearance. He went 220 days in 2022 without doing one TV interview. And when Biden does actually answer a question, oftentimes it's a lie.

"Do you take any blame for inflation, Mr. President?" a reporter asked in January 2023 as he tried to leave the podium after a speech that was the verbal version of twerking regarding how great he thought the economy was.

"Do I take any blame for inflation? No," Biden replied, visibly annoyed by the question.

"Why not?" the reporter followed.

"Because it was already there when I got here, man," he responded with an obvious lie. "Remember what the economy was like when I got here? Jobs were hemorrhaging, inflation was rising. We weren't manufacturing a damn thing here. We were in real economic difficulty. That's why I don't. Thank you."

There would be no other questions.

So to unpack this, Biden claimed inflation "was already there" when he arrived. It sure was, clocking in at just 1.4 percent when Trump left office. When Biden made this claim, inflation was nearly *five times higher* at 6.5 percent. Wages, of course, were not keeping up with inflation.

This is one of hundreds of examples of Biden gaslighting and getting away with it. That helps when pious fact-checkers, who were ubiquitous on television during the Trump era, are on a four-year spring break. Democrats have become so bold that one former senator turned MSNBC pundit, Claire McCaskill, declared on *Morning Joe* the following: "I move that every newspaper in America quits doing any fact checks on Joe Biden!"

She really said that. And Joe and Mika just nodded along. . . .

If looking for other examples of why it's so awesome to be a Democrat, just ask Sen. Elizabeth Warren (D-MA), who lied on a job application about her Indian heritage that did not exist. Any Republican would have been driven out of town after such a revelation. But no such thing happened. Instead, many media members somehow defended Warren despite her DNA showing she had somewhere between a whopping $1/64$ and $1/1,024$ Native American DNA.

"Warren's Native American DNA, as identified in the test, may not be large, but it's wrong to say it's as little as $1/1,024$th or that it's less than the average European American," concluded the *Post* after Trump tweeted out the $1/1,024$ number. And they were serious.

The Facts on Elizabeth Warren's DNA Test—FactCheck.org:

Claim: *Sen. Elizabeth Warren "doesn't have any Indian blood."*

Claimed by: *Donald Trump.*

Fact-check: *False.*

False?? What. The. Actual. F***?

NBC News: *"Elizabeth Warren releases DNA Results Indicating She Has Native American Heritage: Trump, Who Has Said He Would Donate $1M to Charity if Warren Took a DNA Test, Replied Bluntly to the News: 'Who Cares?'"*

So you see, because Trump led the charge against Warren's BS claim, that triggered the reflex for "fact-checkers" and so-called news organizations to make *Warren* the victim.

"She has a fraction of a fraction of Indian DNA, therefore Trump is lying!"

You can't make this stuff up.

It really is good to be a Democrat.

Here's another reason. If I taught a class on just how corrupt our media has become, here's the ultimate example: comparing coverage of two horrific tragedies and how the president at the time was treated.

The year was 2005. In August, Hurricane Katrina, a Category 4 hurricane, slammed into New Orleans and killed fourteen hundred people. When the storm hit, President George W. Bush was on the annual vacation leading up to Labor Day weekend that all presidents in the modern era take during the unofficial end of summer.

On his way back to Washington after the storm hit, Air Force One flew over New Orleans to allow Bush to look over the damage. Photographers on the plane snapped away as Bush, sitting alone, looked out the window at the devastation. By his own admission in his 2010 memoir, this was a decisive moment for Bush, who once had a 90 percent approval rating after 9/11.

"I barely noticed the photographers at the time. I couldn't take my eyes off the devastation below. But when the pictures were released, I realized I had made a serious mistake. The photo of me hovering over the damage suggested I was detached from the suffering on the ground," he wrote. "My heart broke at the sight of helpless people trapped on their rooftops waiting to be rescued."

The compassionate conservative was elected twice because, some would say, he connected with people and seemed like a regular guy who cared about all Americans. The infamous image of Bush peering out the plane window down at the ruin Katrina had inflicted dropped like a bomb. The outrage from the media was hostile to the point of personal.

The *New York Times* said Bush critics characterized the flyover as "an imperial act removed from the suffering of the people below."

USA Today: *"A Compassionate Bush Was Absent Right after Katrina"*

CBS News: *"What if They Were White?"*

Enter Kanye West, who in 2005 was a hugely successful hip-hop artist who wasn't remotely seen as a political activist or anyone who shared opinions of current events very much. Remember, this was a pre-Twitter world, before our current state of communications where anyone and everyone can share every inane thought in their head without a buffer and send out to millions in a flash for free.

"George Bush doesn't care about Black people," Kanye said while standing next to Mike Myers during a nationally televised MTV telethon.

Since this was years before Kanye had aligned himself with Donald Trump, Kanye was hailed as a courageous hero by multiple media members and pundits for saying such a thing. Bush was a Republican president, after all. And Kanye, who in 2022 turned out to be a Holocaust denier and full-fledged anti-Semite, was simply a caring person standing up for his people.

"I faced a lot of criticism as president. I didn't like hearing people claim that I lied about Iraq's weapons of mass destruction or cut taxes to benefit the rich. But the suggestion that I was racist because of the response to Katrina represented an all-time low," Bush told NBC's Matt Lauer. "I still feel that way. I felt [that way] when I heard [those words], felt them when I wrote them, and I felt them when I'm listening to them. It's one thing to say, 'I don't appreciate the way he's handled his business,'" he said. "It's another thing to say, 'This man's a racist.' I resent it, it's not true."

Good for Bush. This was a president who selected the first Black person to serve as secretary of state (Colin Powell) and the first Black female to take on the same role (Condi Rice). Bush was a flawed president. But to call the guy who saved millions of lives in Africa due to his $1.2 billion Malaria Initiative . . . a racist over Katrina? Please.

Fast-forward to August 2023: Wildfires engulf the island of Maui, causing mass devastation that leads to hundreds dead, making it the deadliest fire in US history. Sirens that are supposed to be triggered never go off. Officials send text message warnings that never get to many who need them because power and cell towers are already down.

President Joe Biden, having returned on August 7 to the White House from a ten-day vacation at his beach house in Rehoboth, Delaware, is back at his beach house on August 11 for four more days of rest and relaxation as reports continue to bring in profoundly grim news out of Maui.

For days, the commander in chief has not made any public comments. But on Sunday, Bloomberg reporter Justin Sink posts the following on X, the newly branded version of Twitter:

"After a couple hours on the Rehoboth beach, @potus was asked about the rising death toll in Hawaii. 'No comment,' he said before heading home."

Wait . . . no comment?

No comment?

Nothing about thoughts and prayers for the residents of Maui?

Nothing about the federal government providing all the resources it can in the search for the missing?

No updates on what FEMA is providing on the ground?

No federal investigation to announce why warning systems failed?

Nothing about asking Americans to donate in this time of need?

No comment?

Sink's post, which was viewed more than ten million times, included a photo of Biden sitting on the beach with the First Lady and others. Later that same day, when reporters asked again about the rising death toll on Maui, Biden stared for a moment at the press pool before again responding, "No comment." Then he smiled before getting into his motorcade.

Things got worse when Biden, upon meeting with Maui residents at a time when hundreds were reportedly missing, decided to broach yet another lie about a small fire at his home twenty years before.

"I don't want to compare difficulties, but we have a little sense, Jill and I, what it's like to lose a home," he said. "Years ago—now 15 years ago—I was in Washington doing 'Meet the Press.' It was a sunny Sunday, and lightning struck at home on a little lake that's outside of our home—not a lake, a big pond—and hit a wire and came up underneath our home into the heating ducts—the air conditioning ducts.

"To make a long story short, I almost lost my wife, my '67 Corvette, and my cat."

The Cranston Heights Fire Company, which extinguished the fire at Biden's home, said at the time that it was "an insignificant fire" and "did not lead to multiple alarms and did not need a widespread incident response throughout the county."

The flames were confined to the kitchen, the fire chief said, and were under control in under twenty minutes.

At a ceremony honoring Maui fire victims that same day, Biden proceeded to doze off for a good twenty seconds.

So to sum it up:

- Biden went on two vacations after the Maui fire began.
- He said "No comment" to reporters asking about updates on two occasions.
- He fell asleep at an event honoring victims.
- He tried to equate a small house fire where no one got hurt to the worst fire in US history in terms of fatalities.

Rest assured—as we saw with George W. Bush, if this were a Republican president acting and speaking this way, cable news personalities would be losing their minds in outrage and condemnation.

And it wasn't just Bush who got a raw deal. Check out the way the press went after President Trump for his actions *before* hurricanes hit the United States.

Washington Post, in 2017: *"Lost Weekend: How Trump's Time at His Golf Club Hurt the Response to [Hurricane] Maria"*

CNN, in 2019: *"Trump Went Golfing as Hurricane Dorian Threatens US"*

New York Daily News, again in 2019: *"Trump Once Again Spends the Day at His Virginia Golf Course as Florida Braces for 'Catastrophic' Hurricane"*

See how this works?

According to the Democratic governor of Hawaii, John Green, 2,200 structures in Maui had been destroyed as a result of the wildfires, with 86 percent of those structures being residential.

At a press briefing held the day before Biden finally left his beach house and went to Maui, White House press secretary Karine Jean-Pierre botched the names of both Democratic US senators from Hawaii and even misgendered one of them, which seemingly is a jailable offense. When asked about the president's response, she attempted to explain that Biden had spoken to Senators Mazie Hirono and Brian Schatz about the situation:

"Sen. Horino, who I've said the president spoke to just last night. He thanked the president for the immediate support the federal agencies have delivered for residents of Hawaii."

Senator Horino is a she.

After that, Jean-Pierre shared the news that Biden would be traveling to the multimillion-dollar Lake Tahoe mansion of billionaire Tom Steyer for a vacation that would last six days while many Maui residents were left homeless.

Ah, it really is good to be a Democrat, especially when you're a Democrat at the annual conference in Davos, Switzerland.

The name of the city itself oozes pretentiousness. Davos is the same shitshow in the Swiss Alps each year, consisting of the most pious "leaders" on the planet here to tell us about the dangers of climate change. In a related story, more than *a thousand private jets* are flown into Davos each year. That alone is a dealbreaker marinated in thick hypocrisy.

John Kerry, the 2004 Democratic nominee who nearly beat George W. Bush, has repeatedly partied on yachts or flown private around the world hundreds of times. As you may have heard, private jets can produce up to fourteen times the emissions of a commercial flight per passenger. Kerry is almost never called out on this by the American press, of course. Instead, he gets the same protection Biden and Buttigieg get. It took an Icelandic reporter named Jóhann Bjarni Kolbeinsson to finally ask Kerry, moments before the Biden Climate Czar accepted an environmental award in Reykjavik, about how he got to the island country:

"I understand that you came here with a private jet. Is that an environmental way to travel?" Kolbeinsson asked a startled Kerry.

"If you offset your carbon—it's the only choice for somebody like me who is traveling the world to win this battle," Kerry responded. Because flying commercial is only reserved for the little guy and gal whom Kerry privately loathes being in close contact with.

"I've been involved with this fight for years. I negotiated with [Chinese] President Xi to bring President Xi to the table so we could get [the Paris Accord]. And, I believe, the time it takes me to get somewhere, I can't sail across the ocean. I have to fly, meet with people and get things done," Kerry said.

No, you can't sail across the ocean, John. But you can fly the middle seat on Delta or United *over* it like I have.

"But, what I'm doing, almost full time," he added, "is working to win the battle on climate change, and in the end, if I offset and contribute my life to do this, I'm not going to be put on the defensive."

The balls on this guy.

Practice what you preach or change your speech.

During and after Maui, the president has never looked so detached, so impersonal, so uncaring. These are the kind of moments that can sink a presidency. And as Bush 43 will tell you, once that impression is made, it's impossible to unring that bell.

Unless, of course, the bell never rings because the media covers for you if you have a (D) next to your name.

It really, really is good to be a Democrat.

CHAPTER 8

King Biden Illegally Forgives Student Loans (in an Effort to Buy Votes)

His name is Jason Furman. Democrat. A former chairman of then president Obama's Council of Economic Advisors. And here's what he had to say about President Biden's Student Debt Relief Plan, which entailed about twenty million students having their debt completely and magically erased.

"Student loan relief is not free. It would be paid for," Furman explained on Twitter in August of 2022. "Part of it would be paid for by the 87% of Americans who do not benefit but lose out from inflation. Part of it would be paid for by future spending cuts [and] tax increases—with uncertainty about who will bear those costs," he correctly added.

Furman's comments would be big news if the shoe was on the other foot. Let's put it this way: let's say President Trump's former chief economic advisor, Larry Kudlow, went on his successful Fox Business program and declared that Trump was wrong about X, Y, Z on a proposal, and here's why. You can be assured those comments would be played on a loop on CNN/MSNBC, while mockery of Trump would rain down on Twitter.

So if this is the first time you're hearing about Furman's perspective on Biden's terrible, horrible, no-good, very bad idea to "cancel" student loan debt, there's a reason for that: the media—outside of a few exceptions like Fox or the *New York Post*—engaged in this thing called the bias of omission, which means to not report something that is newsworthy in an effort to protect a Democrat president.

Congressman Tim Ryan of Ohio is one of those few Democrats who also spoke out against Biden's plan. Here's what he told Sandra Smith and John Roberts on Fox's *America Reports*:

"As someone who's paying off my own family's student loans, I know the costs of higher education are too high," Ryan said. "And while there's no doubt that a college education should be about opening opportunities, waiving debt for those already on a trajectory to financial security sends the wrong message to the millions of Ohioans without a degree working just as hard to make ends meet."

That "trajectory to financial security" Ryan was referring to involves a good chunk of those who would receive loan forgiveness—students who earned advanced or *graduate degrees*. A solid majority of those with grad degrees are doctors and lawyers and economists and mathematicians and political scientists and professors. And what do all of these folks have in common? *They make more than enough effing money to pay back the money they were loaned!*

Excuse the yelling, but this really puts a bee in my bonnet.

My kids are in second and fourth grade. We're still a good eight to ten years before they go off to college. Non–Ivy League schools like Stanford, Duke, and Georgetown all cost more than $80,000 per year all-in. That's $320,000 for four years. We live in New Jersey, where state income taxes are the fourth-highest in the country. So we're talking about earning *$600,000 before taxes* just to send one kid to these kinds of schools.

This is insanity. And it's only going to get worse.

Jessica Chasmar of Fox Business reported that, "according to the Penn Wharton Budget Model, the handout will cost around $300 billion for taxpayers and will increase to around $330 billion if the program is continued over the standard 10-year budget window."*

But here's the bigger issue, per Ben Ritz of the Progressive Policy Institute's Center for Funding America's Future: "Incoming and future students would in fact be the biggest losers of large-scale debt cancellation because of its impact on inflation," wrote Ritz in *Forbes*.

> Money that would be spent on payments that have been either suspended or cancelled are instead being used to bid up the price of goods and services already facing sharp inflationary pressures. As a result, the Federal Reserve will have to raise interest rates even higher than they otherwise would have to stabilize prices. In other words, broad debt cancellation benefits high-income people who borrowed for their degrees in past years at the expense of higher costs to younger borrowers who already have to pay more than their predecessors because of skyrocketing tuition.

Couldn't have said it better myself. Democrats—the alleged party of the little guy—couldn't give two shits about that single mom who works two jobs or that firefighter or cop risking their life who may not have attended college at all, or even the steel mill or construction worker who also went straight from high school into the workforce. Overall, 62 percent of adult Americans didn't attend college at all. Where's *their* bailout?

Truth is, only 34.8 percent of Americans have a bachelor's degree, while only 13.8 percent have earned a graduate degree. And these are the folks the Biden administration is catering to, the ones who mostly don't need this "forgiveness" in the first place, all while that waiter or cop or fireman or construction or steel mill worker doesn't receive one dime from the federal government for the crime of not attending college.

---

* Jessica Chasmar, "Biden's Student Loan Handout to Cause Spike in College Tuitions, Experts Say," Fox Business, August 24, 2022, https://www.foxbusiness.com/politics /bidens-student-loan-handout-cause-college-tuitions-spike-experts-say.

In a related story, less than 10 percent of student loans are held by the bottom third of earners. Oh, and future college students will get hosed as well through higher costs.

And for what? So Biden and Democrats can improve their standing with younger voters. Thankfully, the Supreme Court stepped in and ruled 6–3 that Biden's gambit was unconstitutional. Because of course it is. Just ask Nancy Pelosi, who once said, "People think that the president of the United States has the power for debt forgiveness. He does not. He can postpone. He can delay. But he does not have that power. That has to be an act of Congress."

For once, she makes sense.

"The question here is not whether something should be done; it is who has the authority to do it," Chief Justice John Roberts correctly wrote in this opinion. And it really is that simple: the president cannot wave billions of dollars away with a magic wand without the consent of Congress, which controls the purse strings. Period.

But if Team Biden thinks the student loan forgiveness gambit is helping them with young voters, they should think again. Multiple polls in 2024 show Trump leading Biden among voters under thirty-five. Going into the 2020 election, Biden led Trump in the same category by an average of 16 points. The bottom has dropped out. Because maybe, just maybe, those who didn't go to college or have paid off their loans know a bribe when they see one.

Despite the Supreme Court decision that Biden's forgiveness Ponzi scheme was completely illegal, through the spring of 2024, the president who insists he is the man who will ultimately protect democracy from the *eeeeevil* Donald Trump keeps ramming through billions of dollars in forgiveness (as in, we all get to pay for the loans provided to others) via executive order. It's the stuff of dictatorship in an effort to maintain power. And it's such horseshit, it sticks to your boots.

We've all heard the term *limousine liberals*, but we're going to take it one step further in our next chapter. Ladies and gentlemen, meet the champagne socialists!

CHAPTER 9

The Champagne Socialists

The future congresswoman—dressed in all white that set off her deep red lipstick, expensive Movado watch, and flowing dark hair right out of a beauty salon—fought back tears at the sight of kids in cages at the southern US border. And most of the American media wept along with her while directing their anger at then president Trump.

It is amazing looking back on this photo just how, well, perfect it is. The previously unknown twentysomething Alexandria Ocasio-Cortez, a former bartender supposedly with little money while running for a congressional race against ten-term congressman Joe Crowley, bucked climate change and flew down to the US-Mexico border to see first-hand how illegal migrants were being treated by the Trump administration. And at the exact moment when her emotions broke down to the point that her body gave way, a professional photographer just happened to be right there to capture this historic moment.

But some critics pointed out that maybe, just maybe, this photo was staged. AOC was so unknown at the time that even her hometown paper, the *New York Times*, barely mentioned her in the lead-up to victory. The "paper of record" was even called out by its own readers for ignoring her to the point that the *Times* local editor had to offer up some lame excuses.

"Our heavy, competing demands for coverage make it impossible to do all the stories we want to do, including all the ones we see and all the ones that we don't see clearly because of the surprise factor," explained politics editor Patrick Healy. "I do wish I had assigned a piece that fully captured the dynamics, demographics and issues in the Ocasio-Cortez/Crowley race before Primary Day on Tuesday. I took away some lessons here."

So the *New York Times* basically missed the AOC train, but a photographer somehow sensed she was a big enough deal before her election put her on the map to snap some awesomely choreographed photo two thousand miles from her home? Hey—makes sense to me.

Some pundits and pollsters see AOC as a future president. And, no, not president of TikTok, but the actual president of the United States. Her stance on climate change and taxing the rich make her at least the next Bernie Sanders, the guy who nearly captured the party nomination in 2016.

AOC took her socialist mantra to a whole new level in September 2021 when she attended a $35,000-per-ticket gala at the Metropolitan Museum of Art. Dressed all in white again, the lawmaker also had painted "Tax the Rich" in large letters on the back of her gown, the creation of Aurora James, a big deal in fashion design. Social media erupted as the usual hacks in media cheered.

CNN: *"AOC Caused a Stir with Her Statement-Making Met Gala Gown"*

Elle: *"Alexandria Ocasio-Cortez's Met Gala Gown Comes with a Strong Message: Tax the Rich"*

GQ: *"AOC's 'Tax the Rich' Dress Was Precision-Engineered Met Gala Messaging"*

Mercury News: *"AOC Launches 'Tax the Rich' Political Merchandise off Met Gala 2021 Dress Controversy"*

Yup. No mention that her "Tax the Rich" sweatshirt cost $58, and the tote bag went for $27, while stickers were somehow $10. The socialist was officially a capitalist. And not one headline with the word *hypocrite* in it from traditional media or the fashion magazines that mocked and/or shunned an actual former model turned First Lady in Melania Trump. In a related story, the designer of AOC's gown, Aurora James, was later revealed to having owed tens of thousands of dollars in back taxes in multiple states. So much for taxing the rich.

Oh, and this event occurred while New York still required masks to be worn in museums, all while not having such a rule for eighteen thousand people screaming at Knicks and Rangers games at Madison Square Garden. AOC, despite being the Queen of Virtue Signaling, wore no mask, while all the workers there were required to do so.

Don't know about you, but the pandemic was truly the stupidest and . . . what's the word we're looking for here? Ah, right . . . most *hypocritical* time of our lives when it came to Democrats breaking their own rules time and time and time again.

AOC represents the Bronx as part of her district. So let's say you're a single mom who works as a teacher there. The average annual salary is $65,840, according to Salary.com, meaning that with New York's high taxes on top of federal taxes, you're taking home about enough money to enjoy one ticket to a gala AOC enjoyed for free.

But let's say teaching has worn you out and you need to increase your salary because the average cost of a two-bedroom apartment in the Bronx, which will never be confused with Manhattan, is nearly $3,000 per month. And then let's say you're excited to hear that Amazon is planning to bring a huge hub to your congresswoman's district.

The year was 2019. Amazon's plan was to hire 25,000 to 40,000 workers at an average salary of $150,000 per year. This was truly an exciting moment for many of AOC's constituents.

Until she killed the deal. And to this day, she celebrates doing so.

"$0 for schools. $0 for firefighters. $0 for infrastructure. $0 for research and healthcare," AOC tweeted at the time. "Why should corporations that contribute nothing to the pot be in a position to take billions from the public?

"If we were willing to give away $3 billion for this deal, we could invest those $3 billion in our district, ourselves, if we wanted to. We could hire out more teachers. We can fix our subways. We can put a lot of people to work for that amount of money if we wanted to," she added.

We're governed by children, kids. And remember, this person apparently has an economics degree from Boston University and graduated cum laude. Really.

For starters, why is it a private company's obligation to provide money for schools, firefighters, infrastructure, research, and health care? Amazon would have received $3 billion in *tax incentives* for the deal, but that's an immensely fair trade given the *$27 billion in new tax revenue* the deal was projected to generate (a 9-to-1 ratio). But in AOC's brain, the $3 billion represented a magic pot of money just sitting around, waiting to be spent by the government on what they deemed important.

Three years later, in March of 2023, she was still crowing about it.

"When I opposed this Amazon project coming to New York bc it was a scam of public funds, the whole power establishment came after us. Billboards went up in Times [Square] denouncing me. Powerful pols promised revenge. Op-Eds & CEOs insulted my intelligence," she tweeted. "In the end, we were right."

Despite this unhinged perspective, don't expect AOC to be going anywhere. She could still be serving in Congress until she's Maxine Waters's age. And the media adores her. CNN even gave her a friggin' documentary episode, something it would never dream of giving to a prominent Republican female lawmaker. Per the network announcement in 2021:

CNN will air *Being... AOC*, the first episode of the new series *Being...* from Dana Bash on Monday, August 9 at 9pmET ... In the first episode, Bash speaks to Representative Alexandria

Ocasio-Cortez, who gives one of her most personal on-camera interviews to date, opening up about her unique perspective on power and femininity, what drives her, and how threats against her and her previous experience with sexual assault impacted her perspective on January 6th.

One would think CNN's AOC-Fest would have focused on her biggest "achievement": making sure New York didn't become the next major technology hub. Making sure those struggling to get by in a city besieged by rising crime (thanks to lax bail policies that AOC supports) and rising taxes (which AOC also supports) can't get jobs at a company like Amazon, which would have provided some economic comfort to their families while encouraging more companies to come to New York. Instead, the opposite is occurring.

"I had a project in upstate New York behind the grid in Niagara Falls for electricity—a global data center we were building. Eventually it got so bad with the politicians in the local region and the state policy, we moved it to Norway and all the jobs," explained *Shark Tank* host Kevin O'Leary in a March 2023 CNN interview.

"That's New York. Uninvestable," he declared. "Sorry, don't shoot the messenger. Just telling you the way it is."

O'Leary's entrepreneurship instincts currently put his net worth at more than $400 million. When CNN anchor Kaitlan Collins retorted that elected officials would disagree with O'Leary's assessment, he didn't hold back: "I'll debate them any time of the day you want, particularly AOC. She's great at killing jobs. She kills jobs by the thousands."

Fact-check: True.

Democrats used to be all about being the party that championed the blue-collar worker. But today it's about representatives like AOC attending galas that cost $35,000 per ticket.

By the way, what AOC did that night at the Met in accepting that ticket—and other gifts, including her dress, handbag, shoes, jewelry, hair, makeup, and transportation—was probably against the law, according to the Office of Congressional Ethics. But don't expect an apology. That simply isn't in her DNA.

It was Bernie Sanders's 2016 presidential run that marked AOC's first foray into politics as an organizer for the campaign. Perhaps it was here that she learned how to say one thing, only to do the complete opposite.

Bernie, as we know, embraces socialism. Wears it on his sleeve. He deplores the rich. That's fine, except Mr. Sanders really likes to fly private. A lot.

"I'm not shocked that while thousands of volunteers braved the heat and cold to knock on doors until their fingers bled in a desperate effort to stop Donald Trump, his Royal Majesty King Bernie Sanders would only deign to leave his plush D.C. office or his brand new second home on the lake if he was flown around on a cushy private jet like a billionaire master of the universe."

That's not a quote from some MEGA-MAGA supporter but from Zac Petkanas, the director of rapid response for the 2020 Clinton campaign when Bernie was making Hillary's coronation to the nomination very uncomfortable.

Sanders, a multimillionaire who owns three homes, would go on to write a book called *It's Okay to Be Angry about Capitalism*. And to promote said book, he hosted an event in Washington, DC, where tickets for the anticapitalism event went for as much as *$95* on that evil capitalist company Ticketmaster. Tickets priced $55 or higher included a copy of the book. Nothing says socialism like guaranteed sales! Here's the best part: Bernie made $170,000 in royalties for his book, or about the same he makes annually serving as a senator . . . a position he uses to attempt to destroy the very system that has made him the Daddy Warbucks of the upper chamber.

This book really does write itself.

"Democratic socialism means that we must reform a political system that is corrupt, that we must create an economy that works for all, not just the very wealthy," Sanders once declared.

From the looks of it, things have worked out quite well for Bernie.

Nancy Pelosi, also a media darling—as evidenced by her HBO series *Pelosi in the House*—is another example of "Rules for thee, not for Ds." The former House Speaker and her husband, Paul, are worth more than $114 million. And we've looked at Paul's stock trades over the years; we haven't seen anyone with this kind of Wall Street prowess since that infamous insider trader Gordon Gekko.

"Year after year, politicians somehow manage to outperform the market, buying and selling millions in stocks of companies they're supposed to be regulating," Sen. Josh Hawley (R-MO) declared in 2022. "Here's something we can do: ban all members of Congress from trading stocks and force those who do to pay their proceeds back to the American people."

But Nancy Pelosi had a big problem with this, for some odd reason. "We are a free-market economy. They should be able to participate in [trading stocks]," she declared when asked if she would support such a measure. Even after some bipartisan blowback, Pelosi still maintained that she just didn't "buy into it," but "if members [of Congress] want to do that, I'm OK with that."

That seems like the kind of answer an exhausted parent gives to a child asking for a second dessert.

The Speaker went on to say that she didn't believe the step was necessary because she trusted her colleagues to do the right thing. "I have great confidence in the integrity of my members," Pelosi said. And she was serious.

Meanwhile, Gallup finds that just *2 percent* of voters have a "great deal" of trust in Congress. Gas station sushi is more trusted.

Paul Pelosi's portfolio has substantially outperformed the S&P 500. In 2020 alone, when the stock market was as turbulent as in any year in recent memory thanks to COVID-19 shutdowns, Paul outperformed the S&P 500 by *14.3 percent*, according to Hawley's office. And per a *New York Post* analysis, the Pelosis have made approximately $30 million from trades involving Big Tech companies the House Speaker is responsible for regulating.

This is all just a coincidence, right?

In fact, Paul is so good that there's an app that allows the public to follow his stock trades. And for good reason: the Pelosis' reported net worth is more than $114 million, according to OpenSecrets.org.

Per a *Business Insider* report, "a vast majority of the couple's wealth is derived from stocks, options, and investments made by Paul Pelosi."

In March 2021 Paul exercised options to purchase twenty-five thousand Microsoft shares worth more than $5 million. Less than two weeks later, the US Army disclosed a $21.9 billion deal to buy augmented reality headsets from Microsoft. Shares in the company rose sharply after the deal was announced.* The instincts on this eighty-two-year-old would make Nostradamus blush.

For another purchase in June 2022, Paul gobbled up to $5 million in stock options (equal to twenty thousand shares) of Nvidia, a leading semiconductor company. The purchase, first reported by the *Daily Caller*, came as Congress was set to vote on legislation later that month that would result in $52 billion in subsidies allocated to elevate the chip-production industry as it faced increased competition from China.

So how does the House Speaker explain such a huge buy by her husband so perfectly timed ahead of this vote?

"These transactions are marked 'SP' for Spouse. The Speaker has no prior knowledge or subsequent involvement in any transactions," Nancy's spokesperson explained recently.

But if Paul Pelosi makes money in the stock market, wouldn't his spouse also benefit? The explanation inspires little confidence, but at least these trades are inspiring the House and Senate to act to try to

---

* Miranda Devine, "Stock Raving Mad: The Pelosis' Have an 'Inside' Track—and It Must End," *New York Post*, July 20, 2022, https://nypost.com/2022/07/20/the-pelosis-trading-individual-stocks-must-stop/.

prevent it from happening again. And, of course, the $52 billion bill to boost US semiconductor manufacturing passed.

Meanwhile, Paul Pelosi continues to have the magic touch. On June 17 he exercised two hundred call options (twenty thousand shares) on Nvidia. The stock closed at $158.80 that day. On Friday, July 22, it closed at 173.19. To quote Karen Smith in *Clueless*, it's like he has ESPN or something.

And in November 2023, it happened *again*: Paul placed $2.5 million in call options on Nvidia. And, lo and behold, the company announced a deal for AI chips to be sold in China. A few weeks later, the US government announced Nvidia was selected to be one of several companies it would partner with "to create a national resource for researchers and educators to access high-powered AI technologies with the goal of ensuring the US continues to lead in AI research and innovation," according to a report in Yahoo Finance.

I mean, what are the odds, right?

In an interview with Fox News, Christopher Josephs, the cofounder of Autopilot, an app that offers investors the ability to track a politician's trades, said that the Pelosi investment netted them approximately $1.25 million after Nvidia stock jumped 50 percent in the three months from November 2023 to February 2024. In the end, members of Congress have access to a lot of sensitive information that can help make them seriously richer.

"The most valuable commodity I know of is information," the fictional Gordon Gekko once declared.

And members of Congress certainly have information we don't: inside knowledge of new laws and government deals coming down the pike.

Paul Pelosi would go on to get arrested for a DUI in 2022 after leaving a fancy restaurant in wine country and crashing his Porsche into another car. Officers said his speech was slurred and there was a strong odor of alcohol on his breath. C'mon, this guy can't afford Uber? Such hubris. He would receive a slap-on-the-wrist probation instead of jail time from California's totally uncompromised legal system.

Fortunately, under the GOP-controlled Congress, something may finally get done about insider stock trading by members of Congress. "The PELOSI Act will: Prohibit members of Congress and their spouses from holding, acquiring, or selling stocks or equivalent economic interests during their tenure in elected office," reads the proposed legislation in the Senate from Josh Hawley.

Amen to that.

And if Paul Pelosi is Gekko, then Hillary Clinton is the Billy Ray Valentine of commodities trading.

You remember Billy Ray (Eddie Murphy) of *Trading Places* fame. He's the poor con man pulled off the streets of Philadelphia by Mortimer and Randolph Duke (wonderfully played by Don Ameche and Ralph Bellamy, respectively). Mortimer bets Randolph one dollar that he can transform Billy Ray into a successful executive at their commodity trading firm while at the same time turning the snooty Ivy Leaguer Louis Winthorpe (the perfectly cast Dan Aykroyd) into a criminal by putting him into Billy Ray's poor environment. Spoiler alert on a movie that came out forty-one years ago: Mortimer wins the bet. I could do a whole book on one of the best comedies ever, but that's for another time.

Back to nonfiction, the year was 1978. Future First Lady, senator, and secretary of state Hillary Clinton was a practicing lawyer, while her husband was Arkansas attorney general. The thirty-one-year-old Hillary's income at the time was approximately $25,000 when she suddenly decided to open a commodities/futures account with a $1,000 deposit.

Going purely on her instincts, her first trade out of the gate was the short sale of ten live-cattle contracts. A short sale, of course, is betting that the price of x will go down. Short sales were and are patently uncommon among rookie investors, but here was Hillary Valentine rolling the dice. And on cue, her first trade generated (checks notes) a 530 percent profit.

Over the next year, the future twice-failed presidential candidate racked up $99,541 in profits, with her last two trades also being short sales that netted big returns. Note: When adjusted for inflation, $100,000 in 1978 is worth more than $450,000 today.

A final check of the scoreboard shows Hillary finishing with a pantsuit-popping 10,000 percent return on her initial $1,000 investment. For context, Hillary's performance was *80 times better* than George Soros's in his best year. Soros, of course, made most of the money that he uses to destroy American cities through short-term trading.

"It's not the big banks that need relief from Washington—it's small banks and small businesses," Clinton said during her 2016 campaign. "We should be doing more to rein in risky behavior on Wall Street and 'Too Big to Fail.'"

Risky behavior like . . . short-selling cattle commodities?

"So-called activist shareholders can have a positive influence on companies. It's a good thing when investors put pressure on management to stay nimble and accountable, or press for social and environmental progress," Clinton also said in a 2015 campaign speech. "But that's very different from these hit-and-run activists whose goal is to force an immediate payout—no matter how much it discourages and distracts management from pursuing strategies that would add the most long-term value for the company. . . . So we need a new generation of committed long-term investors to provide a counter-weight to the hit-and-run activists," she concluded.

And if you're looking for a belly laugh, check this out on her 2016 campaign platform: "Hillary would impose a tax on harmful high-frequency trading and reform rules to make our stock markets fairer, more open, and transparent."

In looking at the coverage of Hillary's 2016 campaign against Trump, it is impossible, outside of the *Wall Street Journal*, Fox News, and some online conservative publications, to find one reporter/journalist doing their job correctly on this front. Because how can you possibly cover Clinton's faux stance on "taking on Wall Street" and short-term "hit-

and-run" activists and *not* mention that she made what amounted to nearly *half a million dollars* engaging in this behavior?

Also note: In 1978–79, cattle markets were experiencing their biggest bull market in history, yet Hillary's three most profitable trades that year were from the short side. Remember, she was only making about $25,000 per year working for Rose Law Firm, while Bill was making about $26,000 as Arkansas attorney general. So let's say she *lost* $100,000 shorting these commodities. How exactly would she have covered her bets? Unless, you know, she knew the outcome.

This all reminds me of an old friend of mine who was part of a college basketball point-shaving scandal while at Arizona State. After having assurance from the team's star player (Stevin "Hedake" Smith) that he would make sure the opposing team covered the spread through missed shots, free throws, and timely turnovers, he and his partner flew to Vegas and bet a fortune on the Sun Devils over the course of several games. If you *knew* the outcome of a bet before the game was even played (think Biff Tannen being in possession of a future sports almanac in *Back to the Future 2*), wouldn't you put your entire life savings on it?

Rhetorical question.

So did Hillary allegedly ascertain inside information not known to regular investors?

Well, Hillary's top advisor and friend at the time, James Blair, was counsel to Tyson Foods, the largest exporter of beef in the United States and Arkansas's biggest employer. Blair, in a 1994 interview with the *New York Times Magazine*, confirmed that he encouraged Clinton to invest in risky commodity markets but denies any wrongdoing.

Also per that 1994 *New York Times* article: "Mr. Blair and the Administration officials estimated Mrs. Clinton's profits at $100,000. The officials said she opened her trading account in mid-October 1978, three weeks before Mr. Clinton was elected with 63 percent of the vote. She got out of the market on Oct. 17, 1979, just as the rising market in cattle futures from which she had profited was collapsing."

Going into the 2016 election, we heard a lot from *New York Times* executive editor Dean Baquet about the need to see Trump's tax returns. Baquet even went so far to say *he would risk jail time* if that meant the publication getting their hands on the returns and publishing them, which doesn't sound like something a liberal activist would say or anything.

In another, related story, the trades in which Hillary profited the most have never been publicly disclosed. And when the Clintons put down $60,000 on a house in 1980, Hillary said the money from the down payment came from her savings and courtesy of a gift from her parents (personal note: my dad gave me a Weber grill when Mrs. C. and I moved into our first home, and we thought *that* was generous). Bill's 1979 salary as governor was just $35,000.

Hillary would go on to profit from Wall Street again through three lucrative speeches that netted her a cool $675,000 in 2013. And if not for Wikileaks dumping the contents of John Podesta's emails, which included the payments, we would have never known just how attached at the hip Hillary was to eeeeeevil Wall Street despite her bluster to the contrary.

If you wonder how exactly Donald Trump bested Hillary in the 2016 presidential election despite long odds and a media invested in ensuring his failure, it was because this kind of message resonated not just with Blue Dog Democrats and independents but with those who had lost so much faith in our institutions and either major party that they simply didn't bother to vote anymore.

"The forgotten men and women of our country will be forgotten no longer," Trump said in his inauguration speech, which was dubbed "dark," "raw," "weird," and "threatening" by our totally objective media. "And I will fight for you with every breath in my body, and I will never, ever let you down."

Going into this presidential election, the paradigm continues to shift. A 2023 CNBC poll found that America's millionaires are more likely to support Biden over Trump by double-digit margins. The trend is real: following 2016 and 2020, the top 40 percent of income earners preferred Hillary Clinton and Joe Biden, respectively, over billionaire Donald Trump. And in 2012 voters earning $220,000 or more supported Barack Obama over former venture capitalist Mitt Romney.

Democrats weren't always the party of the rich. In the 1980s, polls showed that Republicans earned *70 percent* of the rich vote, while Democrats captured just 15 percent. And does anyone remember Occupy Wall Street in 2011? For two months, unbathed liberals occupied Lower Manhattan. They dubbed themselves the "99 percent versus the richest 1 percent" and captured major media attention across the country by arguing for financial equity following the 2008 crash.

But in this presidential campaign, we're seeing Kamala Harris host what are dubbed "grassroots fundraisers" in places like the blue-collar haven that is Martha's Vineyard for the low, low price of up to $10,000 per plate. It was a step down for Scranton Joe, who spends his Thanksgivings as president at the Nantucket home of private-equity billionaire David Rubenstein, valued at more than $30 million.

"We have to rehire some IRS agents . . . not to try to make people pay something they don't owe—just to say, 'Hey, step up. Step up and pay like everybody else does,'" Biden shouted at his reelection launch at the White House. "Look, I really mean this. Look at my whole career—and I come from, you know, the corporate State of America. I just think it's about just paying your fair share, for Lord's sake."

Biden comes from the corporate state of America? He's been in politics for more than fifty years, since the Vietman War was still raging.

Speaking of war, Democrats used to be the antiwar party. But in 2024, many of them can't seem to get enough of it. On your dime, of course.

CHAPTER 10

The Party of War

"Daisy" changed the game for political advertising and made the element of fear in election ads very nearly an imperative. The message was both frightening and frighteningly simple: LBJ's Republican opponent Barry Goldwater was a hawk and warmonger who would surely lead the U.S. into a nuclear war if elected. Even today, "Daisy," with its juxtaposition of childish innocence and global destruction, feels chilling and astoundingly effective.

What you just read was a review in Salon of a campaign ad that aired during the 1964 presidential race, produced by President Lyndon B. Johnson's campaign team. The liberal publication had released its list of the ten "most fear-mongering political ads" in American political history, and LBJ's "Daisy" topped the list.

Johnson ran on an antiwar, antinukes platform against the hawkish Barry Goldwater, who suggested using nuclear weapons in the escalating Vietnam War in 1963. LBJ's campaign seized on such a suggestion, prompting Goldwater to make one of the more candid confessions a presidential candidate has ever made publicly: "There are words of mine floating around in the air that I would like to reach up and eat," the Republican once said.

Johnson would go on to win in a landslide, winning forty-four of fifty states. But the United States only expanded its mission in Vietnam during the Johnson presidency, and it was his inability to prevent the United States from putting boots on the ground in Vietnam that ultimately led to his stunning announcement on March 31, 1968, that he would not be seeking reelection.

"With America's sons in the fields far away, with America's future under challenge right here at home, with our hopes and the world's hopes for peace in the balance every day, I do not believe that I should devote an hour or a day of my time to any personal partisan causes, or to any duties other than the awesome duties of this office—the presidency of your country," a solemn Johnson announced to the nation. "Accordingly, I shall not seek, and will not accept, the nomination of my party for another term as your president."

Liberals obviously loathed the war in Vietnam and made their voices heard on college campuses and at protests throughout the war. "Peace, Love, Dope!" became a rallying cry around the country. Edwin Starr's anti-Vietnam song "War" practically became a national anthem.

Researching the material for this book has been an educational pleasure because of nuggets like these: Did you know that Michael Dukakis, as a state representative in 1970, staunchly supported a bill that would have exempted Massachusetts residents from fighting in the Vietnam War? The bill said any resident could refuse to partake in "armed hostilities" that were "not an emergency" and "not otherwise authorized in the powers granted to the President as Commander in Chief."

No, this was *really* a bill. The George H. W. Bush campaign team smartly made Dukakis's vote a campaign issue in an effort to portray him as a squishy liberal and therefore the opposite of the current president of the time, Ronald Reagan, and a sharp contrast from Bush 41, a war hero who was shot down during a bombing run over the Pacific in 1944 before being rescued by a US submarine.

But Dukakis overcompensated in what has gone down as one of the biggest turning points a presidential campaign has ever suffered. *Politico* even called it "the worst campaign photo op ever."

Remember, Dukakis was once up 17 points on Bush in August 1988. But then came a photo on September 13 of the diminutive Dukakis smiling and pointing to photographers while wearing military gear over his suit, complete with an idiotic tank commander helmet that read "Mike Dukakis" on it. It just looked so phony, especially considering how dovish Dukakis had always been.

Dukakis never recovered. He went from the clear favorite to winning just ten out of fifty states against Bush, not exactly Mr. Electricity on the campaign trail.

Fast-forward to 2019: President Trump announces his plan to remove US troops from Syria. One would think Democrats would cheer such a move, but a Morning Consult/*Politico* poll shockingly says otherwise. "Of people who voted for Clinton in 2016, only 26 percent support withdrawing troops from Syria, while 59 percent oppose it," it reads. "But Trump voters overwhelmingly support withdrawal by 76 percent to 14 percent."

That is so telling of where the mindset of today's donkeys is on war and peace: a fifty-point margin on the question of pulling troops out of the hotbed to end all hotbeds that was Syria's civil war.

"Why are we sitting silently by and watching him do Putin's bidding?" Hillary Clinton predictably asked PBS about Trump's troop removal plan. "There's no happier man in the world right now than Putin."

Actually, it was during Hillary's tenure as secretary of state that there was no happier man in the world than Putin. Because just a little over one month after she took over as secretary of state, Hillary met with the Russian foreign minister Sergey Lavrov and decided it was a swell idea to present him with a gift. The gift? A cartoonish red button with the words *peregruzka* (Russian for "reset") and *reset* (English for "reset") written on it.

Russia would go on to annex Crimea during the Obama-Biden administration in 2014. But during the Trump administration, Russia did nothing. And when Biden took office, Putin was back at it again with his insidious invasion of Ukraine.

But, sure, Putin wanted *Trump* in charge, and not Obama/Biden/Clinton, amirite?

Anyway, the golden rule to end all golden rules is one we've all heard: When in doubt, always follow the money. And for being the party for the little guy, most Democratic lawmakers have taken Gordon Gekko's "greed is good" mantra to a whole new level.

So if you're wondering why so many Democrats are so gung-ho about sending billions in weapons to Ukraine, please note that between February 1, 2022, when the Russians were amassing thousands of troops on the Ukrainian border, and April 10, after the war was well underway, Raytheon stock climbed by roughly 10 points, Northrop Grumman stock jumped by over 90 points, and Lockheed Martin stock increased by roughly 75 points. At the time, at least twenty members of Congress owned stock in Raytheon and/or Northrop Grumman.

According to Sludge, "an independent, nonprofit news outlet that produces investigative journalism on lobbying and money in politics," per its masthead, the stocks of the top five defense contractors have grown by an average of 900 percent since September 2001, and "at least 47 members of Congress and their families own between $2 million and $7 million of stock in defense companies," according to the report.

War! What is it we're fighting for?

Profits, apparently.

The United States has now blindly sent well over $100 billion to help Ukraine—a profoundly corrupt country—protect its border instead of investing the money here back home. An October 2023 Reuters/Ipsos poll showed that a majority of Democratic voters (52 percent) still support sending weapons to Ukraine, while just 35 percent of Republican voters feel the same way. That's a 17-point gap.

Former Ohio congressman Dennis Kucinich (D) believes he can

pinpoint when the pivot from antiwar principle to profit occurred: "As soon as the Democratic Party made a determination, it could have been 35 or 40 years ago, that they were going to take corporate contributions, that wiped out any distinction between the two parties," Kucinich said in an interview on the Real News Network in 2022. "Because in Washington, he or she who pays the piper plays the tune. That's what's happened."

The Biden administration's military budget is $858 billion for fiscal year 2023. The $858 billion is $45 billion above what the Biden administration had even requested. Why is that? And all of this is happening as Russia and Ukraine are hopelessly locked in a stalemate that could go on until the end of the decade . . . all while US taxpayers continue to foot much of the bill without knowing if the money is truly being allocated to where it's supposed to go.

In March 2024, Biden's national security advisor, Jake Sullivan, announced that Biden would be sending another $300 million in emergency aid to Ukraine and completely circumvented Congress in the process of doing so. If Dems continue to win elections, rest assured we could be hearing about the tenth anniversary of the Russia-Ukraine war with still no end to the stalemate as our country goes broke and our border is less secure than Ukraine's.

In a related story, the United States is currently approaching $35 trillion in debt, yet we continue to fund foreign wars with zero interest in negotiation to help end them. We're currently adding $1 trillion in debt to that number about *every 100 days*.

"Mankind must put an end to war before war puts an end to mankind," John F. Kennedy once said.

But if there's money to be made, all options are suddenly on the table.

Inflation. Crime. Open borders. Perpetual war. How do we return America to greatness? There's really only one way to do that in 2024. But more on that later. . . .

PART III

Remember When Democrats Cared about More than Identity?

Even the Oscars in deep-blue Hollywood are now racist. Terms like *grandfather clause* and words like *master* are also apparently oozing with racism.

Per the *New York Times*: "A wine organization announced in June that it would no longer use the term 'master' to refer to its high-ranking experts. This month, lawmakers in New Jersey said county elected officials should be called 'commissioners' instead of 'freeholders,' a word that dates to a time when only white males could own land. And on Monday, an appeals court in Massachusetts said that it would no longer use the term 'grandfathering' because 'it has racist origins.'"

We've reached ludicrous speed, folks.

A large swath of today's donkeys label everyone and anything through the prism of race and ethnicity and sexual orientation. They say they're defenders of women, yet advocate having biological men compete against biological women in sports.

It's a party that bestows prestigious honors like the Presidential Medal of Freedom to athletes like Megan Rapinoe. Not because of her accomplishments on the pitch, of course, but because she checks off so many woke boxes, refuses to stand for the national anthem despite representing a national team, and says lots of mean things about Donald Trump and conservatives.

But this is also a party that increasingly isn't fond of the Jewish community very much. So the folks who scream that Trump is Hitler are also the most vocal critics of Israel, calling them "occupiers" and responsible for genocide against the Palestinian people despite its citizens being massacred and raped in their own homes on October 7, 2023. The Squad may be media darlings, but they are among the most anti-Semitic people in the country.

"Identity politics is the mother's milk of the Democratic Left," declared the late, great Charles Krauthammer. And we milk this topic for all it's worth in the next section of this book. Hope you're enjoying it so far!

CHAPTER 11

Reparations, without a Clue
How They're Paid For

Reparations: *the act of making amends, offering expiation, or giving*
satisfaction for a wrong or injury
—*MERRIAM-WEBSTER DICTIONARY*

The debate over whether to offer members of the Black community reparations to help make amends for America's dark past is one that falls (like almost everything else) along ideological lines. Per Pew Research, 48 percent of Democrats support it, compared to 49 percent who don't. Ask the same question of those who identify as Republican, and the split balloons to 8 percent support, 91 percent oppose, or an *82-point swing.*

Overall, 68 percent of Americans oppose reparations, while just 30 percent approve. These numbers aren't stopping San Francisco from trying to forge ahead with a plan to pay thousands of the city's Black residents (checks notes) $5 million in reparations to every eligible Black adult.

Per the Associated Press: "Payments of $5 million to every eligible Black adult, the elimination of personal debt and tax burdens, guaranteed annual incomes of at least $97,000 for 250 years and homes in

San Francisco for just $1 a family. These were some of the more than 100 recommendations made by a city-appointed reparations committee tasked with the thorny question of how to atone for centuries of slavery and systemic racism."

You read that correctly: $5 million to every eligible Black adult. Of course, there are teachers and firefighters and police officers—regardless or color—who have worked their entire lives and can't earn that kind of money over decades of service.

Well . . . surely the city's African American Reparations Advisory Committee put major time and energy into applying some kind of mathematical formula to land on such a number. Or did they?

"There wasn't a math formula," African American Reparations Advisory Committee chairman Eric McDonnell told the *Washington Post* in February 2023.

Oh.

"It was a journey for the committee towards what could represent a significant enough investment in families to put them on this path to economic well-being, growth and vitality that chattel slavery and all the policies that flowed from it destroyed."

So just throw a seven-digit number out there and see if it sticks. Check.

Easy question here: Where exactly is this money going to come from? Because at last check, San Francisco is facing a *$1.4 billion* budget shortfall by 2027.

As we know, usually every modern Democrat's solution in these situations is to simply impose another tax on the rich. "The rich must pay their fair share!" is the broken record on this front. In 2018, for example, the top 1 percent of income earners made nearly 22 percent of all income but paid 42 percent of all federal income taxes.

Sounds like they're paying more than their fair share.

But with high-income earners fleeing the Golden State, tax revenue usually taken in by the state continues to be depleted. Per Bloomberg:

"San Francisco, suffering from some of the nation's weakest office occupancies and stubbornly low transit ridership, is now expecting business taxes over the next two years to decline by $179.3 million from previous estimates. Significantly, property taxes—usually a stable revenue source in downturns—are now projected over the same period to drop by $261 million from the earlier forecast."

So the budget gap is nearly three-quarters of a billion dollars, and there's no tax revenue to save the day. Which brings us back to our original question: Where is $5 million per every eligible Black individual coming from? And before you say Governor Gavin Newsom will save the day, consider this, per the *Wall Street Journal*: "The California Legislative Office estimates tax revenue during this fiscal year and the next will likely be $10 billion lower, and the budget gap will likely be about $7 billion larger than the Governor forecasted last month, assuming Democrats restrain spending."

". . . assuming Democrats restrain spending." Like on, you know, paying $5 million per family.

Oh, by the way, did you know that California *never* adopted slavery in its history? Remember, one of the requirements entails being a "descendant of someone enslaved through US chattel slavery before 1865." So one would guess that if we're going to debate the pros and cons of slavery, perhaps turning to the nation's first and only Black president would be a wise idea.

Barack Obama, 2008: "I have said in the past—and I'll repeat again—that the best reparations we can provide are good schools in the inner city and jobs for people who are unemployed." He added,

I fear that reparations would be an excuse for some to say "we've paid our debt" and to avoid the much harder work of enforcing our anti-discrimination laws in employment and housing; the much harder work of making sure that our schools are not separate and unequal; the much harder work of providing job training programs and rehabilitating young men coming out of prison every year; and the much harder work of lifting 37 million Americans of all races out of poverty.

These challenges will not go away with reparations. So while I applaud and agree with the underlying sentiment of recognizing the continued legacy of slavery, I would prefer to focus on the issues that will directly address these problems—and building a consensus to do just that.

Hard to argue with that perspective.

But somewhere along the way, Obama changed his tune, just as he had on gay marriage. Some would call these instances flip-flopping, but many in the media, who serve at the pleasure of the Democratic Party, have another way to describe a Democrat doing a 180 on a position . . .

"EVOLVING on the issue."

It's a sign of maturity and life experience, you see. Republicans still flip-flop, of course. Only Democrats get the evolution treatment.

Anyway, here's what Obama said about reparations in 2021. You don't even recognize the guy compared to 2004 and 2008.

"Are reparations justified? The answer is yes," Obama 2.0 told Bruce Springsteen on his sleep-inducing *Renegades: Born in the U.S.A.* podcast on Spotify in 2021. "There's not much question that the wealth of this country, the power of this country, was built in significant part—not exclusively, maybe not even the majority of it—but a large portion of it was built on the backs of slaves."

If the former president feels this way, where was this sentiment years ago? Did the woke mob get to him? Is he afraid of the backlash he would surely experience on social media?

Kevin Williamson, a brilliant writer, once wrote this for *National Review* on the subject of reparations:

"The economic interests of African Americans, like those of other Americans, are best served by a dynamic and growing economy, preferably one in which the labor force is liberated from the dysfunctional, antique Prussian model of education that contributes so much to black poverty. The people to whom reparations were owed are long dead; our duty is to the living, and to generations yet to come, and their interests are best served by liberty and prosperity, not by moral theater."

Amen.

Getting money for no good reason is something one female soccer star certainly believes in, all while slamming the United States as a misogynist, racist country.

Meet the insufferable female version of Colin Kaepernick: Megan Rapinoe.

CHAPTER 12

President Rapinoe

All eyes were again on Megan Rapinoe after the United States and Sweden played to a 0–0 tie in regulation in the first game of the elimination round of the 2023 World Cup in August of that year. A loss in penalty kicks would mean the two-time defending US champs would be heading home shockingly early in the Round of Sixteen.

Rapinoe, who hadn't scored the entire tournament or even registered a shot on goal, is the ultra-woke corporate face of the team. In the past few years, after deciding to kneel during the national anthem while strongly urging her teammates to do the same (ex-teammate Hope Solo likened it to bullying), the personality-challenged but impossibly politically correct striker still landed major endorsement sponsorships with Nike, Samsung, Visa, and Subway, among others.

Talent had little to do with the decision to pay Rapinoe millions to sell the brand. If it came down to the numbers, teammate Alex Morgan would have scored all of the aforementioned endorsements, given she's the all-time leading US scorer in international goals, despite being years younger than Rapinoe.

Like Colin Kaepernick, Rapinoe is absolutely adored by the press, particularly after she infamously declared she "wasn't going to the fucking White House" days before the US team had won anything in

2019. So why would she ever say such a thing? Because Donald Trump occupied the Oval Office.

Could she have politely declined? Could she have said something media-savvy, like "Hey, we have to win the championship first before we talk about celebrating anywhere"? Nope. Rapinoe is an activist and celebrity first. And the minute she said that, she was the Joy Behar of soccer.

The headlines were neon from there after Rapinoe became a progressive darling:

NBC News: *"Megan Rapinoe Accepts Ocasio-Cortez Invite to House of Representatives after Clash with Trump"*

The *Guardian*: *"Megan Rapinoe Refuses to Back Down over Donald Trump and White House"*

***Vanity Fair*:** *"Mayor Rapinoe? Senator Rapinoe? President Rapinoe? In America's World Cup Heroine, a Political Star Is Born"*

This is thirty-one flavors of stupid.

And, yes, not long after President Biden took office, the America-hating Rapinoe was awarded the Presidential Medal of Freedom at the White House. For what? No sane person is exactly sure, outside of the usual pandering that is on par with the Biden brand, because you *know* Joe had zero idea who she was when he placed that medal around her neck.

Again, this prestigious award, only bestowed to six female athletes *in history* and not one female American soccer player, was given to the person who had recently said:

"I'll probably never put my hand over my heart. I'll probably never sing the national anthem again."

"You can't win a championship without gays on your team. That's science right there!"

"Your message is excluding people," she also said indirectly to Donald Trump in 2019. "You're excluding me, you're excluding people that look like me, you're excluding people of color, you're excluding Americans that maybe support you."

Of course, Trump is the first president ever to have an openly gay cabinet member after he appointed Ric Grenell as acting director of National Intelligence. He also named Ben Carson, who grew up in a poor Black neighborhood with a single mom, as his HUD secretary. And Trump signed into law the First Step Act, a bipartisan criminal justice reform bill, of which Black men are the biggest beneficiaries.

In other words, Rapinoe is your typical attention-seeking, virtue-signaling activist. She simply is guided by her emotions and her elitist bubble, and therefore doesn't take the time to inform herself before opening her mouth.

Yes . . . the athlete who has made millions in the very country she loathes is the oppressed one. Perhaps she can sign with the Saudis as men's megastar Cristiano Ronaldo did in late 2022. Because in that LGBTQ+ paradise, homosexuality is a crime that is punishable by death. . . . As in being *stoned to death.*

But, yeah, America sucks.

Sports figures weren't always woke. Not even close. The most famous and revered of all time (in my book) is Michael Jordan. Six trips to the NBA Finals, six championships. Never needed a Game 7 in the finals to win said championships. Beat Magic and the Lakers in five games. Beat Drexler and the Blazers in six. Beat Payton and Kemp and the Sonics in six. Beat Stockton and Malone and the Jazz in six. Twice. Impossibly clutch. Played through pain and illness. The consummate team leader. And one of the best defenders the game has ever seen (no one talks about this enough). His Chicago Bulls haven't remotely come close to sniffing a title since Chicago Bulls dunce GM Jerry Krause broke up the team after the 1998 championship.

Jordan reportedly once said (he never denied doing so) that "Republicans buy sneakers too" after being asked why he wasn't more outspoken and engaged politically. MJ understood what LeBron James and Steve Kerr and Rapinoe cannot grasp: that the American people simply do not want to be lectured to. And they *absolutely* do not want politics hijacking the escapism that sports provide.

That's not to say athletes cannot exercise their First Amendment right of free speech. Of course they can. But think of the most successful and/ or beloved athletes of our time: the Manning brothers, J. J. Watt, Derek Jeter, the late Kobe, Carli Lloyd, Caitlin Clark, and Lionel Messi (off the top of my head). Yes, you can generate a huge following without constantly wading into controversial political waters.

Note: Yahoo News and YouGov reported in 2023 that nearly 35 percent of Americans have started to watch less sports, primarily due to woke social justice messaging.

Anyway, getting back to Rapinoe's big moment at the 2023 World Cup against Sweden in the Round of Sixteen, here we were, 4:00 a.m. ET on a Sunday summer morning, in a match being played Down Under. With the world watching and the United States up 3–2 in penalty kicks (five successful kicks are needed to win), Rapinoe set the ball on the penalty kick line, glanced up at the goalie . . .

And promptly sailed it far and wide.

As in *not even close*.

After the kick, she would laugh as she ran off the field. The United States would go on to lose to Sweden in a tournament they were heavy favorites to win.

In almost any other year, the United States would still be congratulated by the American public via social media for their impressive run of two straight titles. Instead, the reaction to the loss was almost euphoric by at least half the country: the women's team came home early, and Rapinoe was one of the primary reasons why.

Donald Trump led the charge after Rapinoe's crucial miss, and it was as brutally candid as one would expect.

Trump: *"The 'shocking and totally unexpected' loss by the U.S. Women's Soccer Team to Sweden is fully emblematic of what is happening to our once great Nation under Crooked Joe Biden. Many of our players were openly hostile to America—No other country behaved in such a manner, or even close. WOKE EQUALS FAILURE. Nice shot Megan, the USA is going to Hell!!! MAGA."*

Megyn Kelly: *"I'm thrilled they lost. You don't support America, I don't support you. [Rapinoe] was too focused on her wokeism, it trickled down to her troops, and now they're losers."*

Former US Women's Soccer star Carli Lloyd, who won two World Cups in 2015 and 2019 before retiring early 2023: *"Within our squad, the culture has changed. It was really tough and challenging to be playing these last seven years. To be quite honest, I hated it. It wasn't fun going in. It was only for love of the game, really, for me. I wanted to win and I wanted to help the team, but the culture within the team was the worst I've ever seen it."*

Former US Men's Soccer star Alexi Lalas: *"Don't kill the messenger. This #USWNT is polarizing. Politics, causes, stances, & behavior have made this team unlikeable to a portion of America. This team has built its brand and has derived its power from being the best/winning. If that goes away, they risk becoming irrelevant."*

Whoops. For whatever reason, that Lalas tweet was going *way* over the line for the politically correct geniuses over at CNN. *How dare he* make an obvious observation that all the off-the-field distractions, led by Rapinoe, may have hurt the team's focus and thereby led to the earliest exit in US women's soccer history in the World Cup? So, as revenge, the equally woke Cable News Network decided to compare Rapinoe's stats with Lalas's.

An on-air graphic compared the number of goals Rapinoe had scored throughout her World Cup career (9) with those scored by Lalas (0). It also showed that Rapinoe won the Golden Boot award for leading scorer in a tournament once, while Lalas had obviously never won one. Boom! High fives were surely being slapped over at the network when that roasting aired!

Except one little problem, and I know this having watched something like five hundred soccer matches between my young daughter's and son's games over the past few years: when you're a defenseman, you almost never score in this sport, especially in international competition, when the scoring is invariably low. And that's because defensemen, you know, *defend*. This isn't hockey, where they can pinch up and join the offense. There are no power plays, save for the rare red card. And if they are successful at not only defending but gaining possession, defensemen get the ball to the midfielders and strikers, who carry the attack on *offense* from there.

To put it in American football terms, CNN doing this is like comparing the number of touchdowns Troy Aikman threw to those thrown by Deion Sanders. It's utterly ridiculous.

In a related story, Lalas was named to the US Soccer Hall of Fame in 2014. He also captured an Emmy for sports broadcasting analyzing games for Fox Sports. Otherwise, you got 'em, CNNers!

And so it goes in America in 2023.

We can't even unite behind one of our most successful national teams because of how polarizing sports like soccer have become. They've turned the beautiful game into another partisan food fight on social issues that have absolutely nothing to do with winning, you know, the game.

Americans like their escapism. But going to a baseball game now means being subjected to Sisters of Perpetual Indulgence (a nun-bashing group) on Pride Night at a Dodgers game, as we saw earlier this summer. Fans revolted. Social media lit up. Why do leagues subject themselves to such unforced errors in an effort to be woke?

Last year's World Series was watched by just an average of less than ten million viewers compared to approximately twenty million in 2009. Nearly half the audience: gone.

Having a Bud Light at the park has taken on a whole new meaning after the company decided to jump headfirst into the transgender debate by publicly sending trans activist Dylan Mulvaney a case of the suds and lost 30 percent in sales in the process. Anheuser-Busch may never fully recover.

Women's soccer may now fall into the same category.

It's a dubious one. One where half the country now sees your brand as just another politically correct, woke, anti-American product.

Megan Rapinoe is the face of that brand. She headed off to retirement from the sport. Thank God. But as with Colin Kaepernick, don't expect her to leave the media spotlight or for the glowing headlines to end anytime soon.

In fact, you can expect to see her sign with MSNBC for political analysis. Because hating half of America is the name of the game there, as is screaming "racism" as often as breathing. For donkeys in 2024, forget simply disagreeing with the other side; the party now actively deals in slandering all of them—including Black members—as racist. But as you're about to see, their strategy is already backfiring.

CHAPTER 13

And You Get a Racist!
And You Get a Racist!

"I don't think we can undo the past."

"I don't think quotas are a good idea."

"We are too mixed to begin to divide ourselves on the basis of race or color."

Multiple choice: Which US president made those statements?

a) Ronald Reagan
b) John F. Kennedy
c) George W. Bush
d) Donald Trump

If you answered b because you knew this is a trick question, kudos to you. Yup, that was JFK. And if most Democrats uttered anything close to those words today, the only word that would come to mind is *ostracized* by the party and many in the media.

It once meant something to call someone a racist, especially in the political arena. The charge had an impact because it was used so carefully and so infrequently. And it's not too long ago that calling someone a racist made national headlines.

In the summer of 2019, CNN and MSNBC found that screaming racism and connecting it to everything President Trump said and did could be good for clicks and ratings.

It certainly worked two years earlier, after Trump's "very fine people on both sides" comment following the violent clashes in Charlottesville, Virginia, over the removal of Confederate statues. Trump, of course, was not referring to neo-Nazis as "very fine people," but to those who objected to taking down a statue of Robert E. Lee in general.

"Excuse me, they didn't put themselves down as neo-Nazis, and you had some very bad people in that group," Trump said on August 16, 2017, in response to a reporter's hostile question. "But you also had people that were very fine people on both sides. You had people in that group that were there to protest the taking down of, to them, a very, very important statue and the renaming of a park from Robert E. Lee to another name."

After another question at that press conference, Trump was clear who he was referring to in the "very fine people" category and who he was not.

"I'm not talking about the neo-Nazis and white nationalists because they should be condemned totally."

No matter. The media went loco while also only dishonestly playing a small clip of Trump's comments to make it appear he was somehow praising white supremacists. Joe Biden would later declare that the "very fine people" comment compelled him to come out of retirement to run for president again in 2020. So we now have Joe Biden's terrible, horrible, no-good, very bad presidency based on a lie pushed by Democrats and the media. Great job, everyone!

From Charlotteville on, terms like *racist* and *fascist* and *autocrat* and *Nazi* and *xenophobe* were associated with Trump on CNN and MSNBC on what seemed like an hourly basis for the rest of his presidency. Because after all, why talk about a roaring economy, manufacturing coming home, or ISIS being crushed and the border being relatively secure when you can just get cheap ratings by dividing the country over racial lines?

The race-baiting was even worse on social media. Just check out what Twitter's head of trust and safety (no, really . . . that's the title), Yoel Roth, tweeted about Trump and his administration two days after taking office in 2017:

"Yes, that person in the pink hat is clearly a bigger threat to your brand of feminism than ACTUAL NAZIS IN THE WHITE HOUSE," he wrote on January 22, 2017.

"I'm just saying, we fly over those states that voted for a racist tangerine for a reason," he declared the day after the 2016 election.

"I've never donated to a presidential campaign before, but I just gave $100 to Hillary for America. We can't fuck around anymore," he also said on September 8, 2016.

Again, this clown was in charge of which tweets stayed and which were censored on the social media giant. So anything directed at Trump that portrayed him as a fascist, racist, or xenophobe not only stayed but was likely amplified. Because look who was in charge.

After Joe Biden took office and Trump was off the stage, the woke brigade in the Democratic Party and in academia and in the media decided to go after another target:

The English language.

And basic sanity.

The scene: the University of Washington, located in a state that is home to many, many more Democrats than Republicans. In 2020, Biden won the state by nearly 20 points.

Liberals on campus are all for free speech . . . at least, until it offends them. At that point, a difference of ideas cannot be debated. Instead, speech can and must be eliminated, just as it is on other campuses like Pyongyang University or at the old Twitter headquarters during the Jack Dorsey era.

In 2022, UW released what ironically was called *The Inclusive Style Guide*. And if you think this book is kinda hilarious so far, check out the guide after a few shots of Jägermeister sometime. Because UW may be home to the Huskies, but it's no longer home to words like *grand-father*, *housekeeping*, *minority*, *ninja*, and *lame*.

Not kidding.

Here's the lame explanation around banning use of the word *lame*.

"This word is offensive, even when it's used in slang for uncool because it's using a disability in a negative way to imply that the opposite, which would be not lame, to be superior," the guide states.

OK . . . How about the word *minority*?

"When 'minority' is used to refer to other races or abilities, it is used as a generalized term for 'the other' and implies a 'less than' attitude toward the community or communities being discussed," the guide states.

If you need to put some ice on your head after banging it against a hard object upon reading this, feel free to do so.

OK, how exactly is *grandfather* a "problematic word" again?

"'Grandfather clause' originated in the American South in the 1890s as a way to defy the 15th Amendment and prevent black Americans from voting," the guide explains.

It gets even better when the guide tackles gender-related terms.

"The word 'manpower' is gendered in a way that implies that men are required for a task, when gender is irrelevant to a task's completion," it says.

How about *man-hours*, when talking about the time it takes to complete a task?

"Use of 'man' is not inclusive, and thus sexist. Gender is unnecessary when describing time worked."

Need another ice pack for that head, pal? Just want to make sure you're OK.

Even colors are banned.

"In cybersecurity, colorization of teams is used to differentiate between different roles or personas in a cybersecurity context. For example, the red team is 'offensive security,' [the] white team is 'coordinators or referees,' the yellow team is the builders of software, etc.," the guide says.

But . . .

"Using colors based as racist tropes—labelling 'white' as good, 'black' as bad, 'red' as attackers, or 'yellow' as excluded third parties—is offensive. Also, 'red atomic' surfaces associations to the Cold War and negative relations with Russia, which was often denoted as 'red' and therefore bad because the country was communist."

Human beings actually wrote this!

OK, well, is the term *spirit animal* at least safe? There can't possibly be any negative connotation there, right?

Right?

"Referring to something as your spirit animal is cultural appropriation," the guide explains.

I definitely picked the wrong week to stop sniffing glue. . . .

Down the road at the University of Southern California, it gets even more ridiculous, if that's possible. Because at the home of the Trojans, in a state that went to Biden by a 34-point margin, the School of Social Work thought it was a good idea to ban the word *field*.

"This change supports anti-racist social work practice by replacing language that could be considered anti-Black or anti-immigrant in favor of inclusive language," a memo from the now-former Office of Field Education reads.

"Language can be powerful, and phrases such as 'going into the field' or 'field work' may have connotations for descendants of slavery and immigrant workers that are not benign."

Did I mention I have two kids in grade school? And what feels like every week, Mrs. C. and I are forced to scratch off another school that we will not allow them to go to. The options are few, but the smart money here is that my daughter, Cameron, lands at the University of Georgia, while Liam is off to Texas. Because if Mommy and Daddy are going to pay north of $250,000 for them each for a college education, we have this little thing against them being indoctrinated at such a cost (and, selfishly, I need solid football programs in warm weather to root for).

To be clear, USC didn't completely ban the word *field*—students are still allowed to say it without fear of consequences. But, staying in the Pac-10 (or whatever is left of the conference at this point), Stanford took matters even further with its Elimination of Harmful Language Initiative by removing the word (checks notes) . . . *American.*

That word "often refers to people from the United States only, thereby insinuating that the US is the most important country in the Americas," the document reads.

Did I mention that Stanford currently costs about $80,000 per year to attend?

Can you imagine Daniel Webster traveling through time and proclaiming during a speech on Stanford's campus his most famous quote?

"I was born an American; I will live an American; I shall die an American."

He would likely either be banned from speaking again at that point or arrested by the word police to serve six hours in a safe space. Might be worse than "The Hole" where Warden Norton placed Andy Dufresne after the "How could you be so obtuse?" scene in *Shawshank.*

Thankfully, Stanford decided to reverse course after Fox News and a handful of other outlets not named ABC, NBC, CBS, PBS, NPR, the *New York Times*, or the *Washington Post* reported on the initiative. Dee Mostofi, the university's assistant VP of communications, explained that the guidelines were only intended for "internal use." The EHLI guidelines "will continue to be refined based on ongoing input from the community," she added.

Back in Washington, DC, Democrats were busy *creating* more words for political gain.

"When I become president, Latinx families will have a champion in the White House," proclaimed Sen. Elizabeth Warren during her failed 2020 run.

"The Latinx community won't be othered by Donald Trump. We won't be scared of his racist rhetoric. We will defeat him," declared Rep. Julian Castro during his unmemorable presidential run. I really wonder if, before that tweet, he *ever* uttered "Latinx" in any private conversation in his life.

Yep. *Latinx*. Per *Merriam-Webster Dictionary*, it means "of, relating to, or marked by Latin American heritage: LATINE—used as a gender-neutral alternative to *Latina* or *Latino*."

"For the curious, in Latinx culture children take *both* their parents' names," explains perhaps the most insufferable person in the history of this republic, the Jar Jar Binks of Congress, Rep. Alexandria Ocasio-Cortez. "It's not a 'progressive, new thing.' It's just how some names work. PR hyphenates, others mark differently. Your last name = the families that came together to make you."

But despite the media attempting to prop up *Latinx* and shame those who didn't use it, the term was *not* catching on in the Latino community.

Per *Politico*:

"Only 2 percent of those polled refer to themselves as Latinx, while 68 percent call themselves 'Hispanic' and 21 percent favored 'Latino' or 'Latina' to describe their ethnic background, according to the survey from Bendixen & Amandi International, a top Democratic firm specializing in Latino outreach. More problematic for Democrats: 40 percent said 'Latinx' bothers or offends them to some degree and 30 percent said they would be less likely to support a politician or organization that uses the term."

As one Democratic pollster told the publication: "Why are we using a word that is preferred by only 2 percent, but offends as many as 40 percent of those voters we want to win?"

But instead of simply taking the L, AOC wasn't about to accept defeat. Instead, she turned to Instagram to vent.

"I have a mini-rant about this because there are some politicians, including Democratic politicians, that rail against the term 'Latinx.' And they're like, 'This is so bad, this is so bad for the party,' like blah blah blah."

We're governed by children, folks.

"And like it's almost like it hasn't struck some of these folks that another person's identity is not about your re-election prospects. Gender
is fluid, language is fluid. . . . Don't have to make drama over it," she
added.

Shorter AOC: "Everybody is wrong. I'm right! Kneel before Zod!"

Thankfully, there are still some Democrats, albeit from another era,
who are warning the party about this crap.

CNN's Van Jones, formerly of Team Obama, argued that Democrats are speaking down to voters.

"We're in danger of becoming a party of the very high and the very
low. If you pull out the working class, you have people who are very
well educated and very well off. Those people talk funny. Latinx? I've
never met a Latinx. I've never met a BIPOC. This weird stuff that these
highly educated people say is bizarre. Nobody talks that way at the bar-
bershop, the nail salon, the grocery store, the community center. But
that's how we (Democrats) talk now."

Paul Begala, a former advisor to President Clinton, also sees the danger of Democrats going down Elitism Boulevard.

"Pain-in-the-ass white liberals on Twitter aren't real Democrats," he
observed in October 2022.

And that's so true. If Twitter truly captured the pulse of the American people, AOC would be a frontrunner for the Democratic nomination. She has more social media followers than any lawmaker on Capitol
Hill, despite having been there for less than six years. CNN dedicated
an entire prime-time series to her. *Time* magazine put her on the cover
and called her "The Phenom." And *GQ* puckered up especially big.

"Congresswoman Alexandria Ocasio-Cortez has become the political voice of a generation—and a cultural star whose power transcends
politics," they gushed.

But one nonpartisan study conducted not too long ago found Ocasio-
Cortez to be one of the *least* effective members of the 435 members of
Congress. She has never had one piece of sponsored or cosponsored legis-
lation passed. All foam and no beer. All sizzle and no steak. That's AOC.

So the next time she or Eric Swalwell or Adam Schiff or Dan Rather or Jim Acosta is trending, is that because there's some kind of groundswell of support around something they said? Or . . . is Twitter not remotely indicative of real life?

Here's something that actually happened in real life: Boston mayor Michelle Wu (D) hosted a holiday party in December 2023 that excluded the seven white members of the thirteen-member city council. The name of the party on the invite? "Elected of Color Holiday Party." Really.

Could you imagine even for one moment what would happen if a white mayor of a major city hosted a holiday party that excluded minority members of a city council and allowed only white members to attend? What would MSNBC and CNN be saying about *that*?

This theme extends to college campuses: UC–Berkeley held an exclusive graduation ceremony for Black students. Its commencement speaker? Maxine Waters, of course. Columbia and Harvard also hold graduation ceremonies based on race. That's nice.

For more proof of this prism, just look at the treatment of Senator Tim Scott (R-SC), the only Black Republican to serve in the Senate.

"[Scott] let @LindseyGrahamSC & the sheriffs *dog-walk him* and destroy police reform after pretending to work on it and now he'll *go along with Lindsey's barking-dog racism* against [Supreme Court] Judge Ketanji Brown-Jackson because: he's Tim Scott," tweeted MSNBC election night cohost Joy Reid after Democrats shot down Scott's proposals on police reform.

Nothing to see here: just blatant racism on display.

"Hear me clearly: America is not a racist country," Tim Scott once said in rebutting President Biden's 2022 State of the Union address. "It's backwards to fight discrimination with different discrimination. And it's wrong to try to use our painful past to dishonestly shut down debates in the present. Original sin is never the end of the story. Not in our souls and not for our nation. The real story is always redemption.

"I think many of us believe the same thing. We are not a racist country. There is racism, of course. But it is not remotely as pervasive as Democrats and the media portray it to be. Dems use it to smear their opponents, while much of the media uses it to scare people, thereby driving up ratings," he correctly added.

Case in point: Immediately after Scott's speech was over, #UncleTim began trending on Twitter.

"Uncle Tim," of course, is a play on Uncle Tom, the lead character in the antislavery novel *Uncle Tom's Cabin*. The character Uncle Tom has become synonymous with subservience and self-hatred.

So much for the tolerant left, where diversity is celebrated, except in situations where class acts such as Scott don't carry the same ideology or worldview. And as we've seen increasingly on America's college campuses, the most important diversity of all—diversity of thought—is dismissed in the most pious manner imaginable.

So, given that Twitter is keenly aware of what the most popular topics are on its platform, one would think #UncleTim wouldn't trend for too long. But one hour became another. Then another. Then six hours. Then eleven hours.

Finally, at nearly the twelfth hour, Twitter decided to block the hashtag. But even then, it blamed "an algorithm" for allowing it to trend for so long.

"This algorithm identifies topics that are popular now, rather than topics that have been popular for a while or on a daily basis, to help you discover the hottest emerging topics of discussion on Twitter," the spokesperson said.

Oh, horseshit.

The *Washington Post* even went so far as to fact-check Tim Scott's background in what can only be described as vile journalism. The fact-check, written by the *Post*'s chief fact-checker, Glenn Kessler, centered on Scott's account of his grandfather having to leave school to pick cotton.

The story's headline stated, "Tim Scott often talks about his grandfather and cotton. There's more to that tale."

Kessler went on to examine census records of the Scott family. The hopelessly biased fact-checker would admit in the piece that "census data is historically questionable at best—and at times unreliable," but went ahead anyway.

And lo and behold, Kessler confirmed that Scott's grandfather did leave school in the fourth grade to work on his father's farm to pick cotton.

Not satisfied, however, Kessler carried out his investigation in search of a crime to find that Scott's family was eventually able to obtain large chunks of farmland "against heavy odds."

"Scott's 'cotton to Congress' line is missing some nuance, but we are not going to rate his statements," Kessler wrote.

Usually at this point, Kessler hands out Pinocchios to whoever he is fact-checking on a scale from one to four (with four marking the most egregious of the four). But here, knowing he had found essentially nothing, Kessler declined to give Scott *any* Pinocchios.

Now ask yourself this rhetorical question: Will the *Washington Post* fact-checker be doing a deep dive into how another Black politician, Maxine Waters, can afford a $6 million mansion in California's swanky thirty-seventh congressional district? And why does Ms. Waters live there, and not in the actual district she represents (the forty-third, which isn't exactly home to the rich and famous)?

Or maybe Kessler can get around to a full fact-check of Black Lives Matter, particularly around how some senior members of the organization were able to purchase opulent multimillion-dollar homes in California after the group set fundraising records in 2020. Worth looking under the hood, no?

These fact-checks won't happen, of course. That would be . . . what's the term again? Fair and balanced.

Hollywood is still mostly profoundly liberal. But one Oscar-winning actor has heard and seen enough, to the point he wants to heave. Say hello to Richard Dreyfuss. And this is his opus. . . .

CHAPTER 14

Richard Dreyfuss Gets It

They make me vomit."

"They" is the Academy of Motion Picture Arts and Sciences, who are the people in charge of the Oscars. And the person doing the vomiting is Richard Dreyfuss, best known as Matt Hooper in *Jaws* and/or Elliot Garfield in *The Goodbye Girl*, for the latter of which he deservedly won an Oscar for Best Actor in 1977.

Dreyfuss was once your typical Hollywood celebrity. He was supporting liberal causes and Democrat candidates and was outspoken in doing so. To that end, Dreyfuss almost seemed to revel in playing the conniving senator Bob Rumson, a Republican caricature looking to take down President Andrew Shepherd (D), aptly played by Michael Douglas, in *The American President*.

But in 2004, well before being woke became a thing, Dreyfuss left the Democratic Party. And since that time, he has railed against diversity quotas and the moral preening taking over Tinseltown.

"This is an art form. It's also a form of commerce, and it makes money. But it's an art," Dreyfuss said on PBS in May 2023 regarding the Academy's grand plan of having films meet specific diversity and inclusion standards in order to be considered for Best Picture. "And no one should be telling me as an artist that I have to give in to the latest, most current idea of what morality is.

"What are we risking? Are we really risking hurting people's feelings? You can't legislate that. And—you have to let life be life. And I'm sorry, I don't think that there is a minority or a majority in the country that has to be catered to like that," he added.

Per the *New York Times*, here's a sample of the criteria the Academy is demanding all films meet:

At least one actor from an underrepresented racial or ethnic group must be cast in a significant role.
—or—
The story must center on women, L.G.T.B.Q. people, a racial or ethnic group or the disabled.
—or—
At least 30 percent of the cast must be actors from at least two of those four underrepresented categories.

This is obviously madness. How exactly would James Cameron have made *Titanic*, which basically swept the Oscars in 1997? Because there were almost no minorities on that ship. No LGBTQ+ at that time. The ship's 3,327 passengers and crew had basically been all white folks, save for just one Black passenger. Would Cameron's film not have been nominated if he had ignored these rules?

How about *Goodfellas*? Would Scorsese have required the mob that existed way back when to fill a racial quota?

In the same PBS interview, Dreyfuss defended Laurence Olivier in Shakespeare's *Othello*, where the actor played his leading character in blackface.

Olivier "did it in 1965. And he did it in blackface. And he played a black man brilliantly," Dreyfuss explained. "Am I being told that I will never have a chance to play a black man? Is someone else being told that if they're not Jewish, they shouldn't play the Merchant of Venice? Are we crazy? Do we not know that art is art? This is so patronizing. It's so thoughtless, and treating people like children."

Scarlett Johansson also had enough of political correctness taking over Hollywood after she was slammed on social media for accepting an offer to play a transgender man.

"Acting goes through trends," Johansson said in a recent interview with *As If.* "You know, as an actor I should be allowed to play any person, or any tree, or any animal because that is my job and the requirements of my job. There are a lot of social lines being drawn now, and a lot of political correctness is being reflected in art."

Johansson noted, "Today there's a lot of emphasis and conversation about what acting is and who we want to see represent ourselves on screen. The question now is, what is acting anyway? I feel like it's a trend in my business and it needs to happen for various social reasons, yet there are times it does get uncomfortable when it affects the art because I feel art should be free of restrictions."

Amen. But this kind of candor did *not* sit well with trolls on Twitter and the usual suspects in the media. Only a LGBT actor can play an LGBT character!* That was the rallying cry. I suppose Dustin Hoffman shouldn't have won an Oscar for playing an autistic adult in *Rain Man.* Tom Hanks shouldn't have won his Oscar as a gay man in *Philadelphia.* Heath Ledger and Jake Gyllenhaal should have been nowhere near *Brokeback Mountain.* And Gina Gershon and Jennifer Tilly should never have been bound to play two lesbian robbers in *Bound.*

For a guy like Richard Dreyfuss, who might not have landed roles like *The Goodbye Girl* or *Mr. Holland's Opus* or *Madoff* if not for his performance in *Jaws* (the top-grossing film in 1975 by a country mile), I can't even imagine what he thought when he saw this headline regarding sharks. And a lack of diversity.

---

* Christi Carras, "James Corden's Performance in 'The Prom' Condemned as Homophobic: 'It's Not Brave,'" *Los Angeles Times,* December 14, 2020, https://www.latimes.com/entertainment-arts/movies/story/2020-12-14/james-corden-the-prom-criticism-twitter.

Washington Post, **December 5, 2022:** "Shark Week *Lacks Diversity, Overrepresents Men Named Mike, Scientists Say*"

If you're going to throw this book across the room, please be gentle.

One of my favorite shows in my single days, and I'm man enough to admit this, was HBO's *Sex and the City.* My Hoboken friends would often get together for watch parties on Sunday nights. The show was so well written, so accurate about singledom in New York, *so damn funny*, at least for the first five seasons, before the characters made the natural progression into maturity while entering their late thirties and forties (Miranda and Charlotte getting married, and Samantha actually embracing monogamy with one boyfriend).

In 2022, for God knows what reason, HBO decided to bring *Sex in the City* back nearly twenty years after going off the air in the form of *And Just Like That.*

Having missed the show and feeling nostalgic to see what Sarah Jessica Parker's Carrie Bradshaw and the other characters were up to in their fifties, my wife and I settled in to watch the first few episodes of the new series.

And it was horrific. The writing? Profoundly bad. The characters? Profoundly and hopelessly woke.

Cynthia Nixon's Miranda, the high-powered, pragmatic attorney who was just about as heterosexually active as any single woman could be outside of Kim Catrall's Samantha Jones in the original series, suddenly decides to leave her husband, Steve, and son, Brady, because at nearly sixty *she realizes she's actually a lesbian* and proceeds to date Che, Carrie's nonbinary Black boss.

"*And Just Like That* Ruined Miranda," reads a headline in the *Atlantic* in February 2022.

The PC on steroids doesn't stop there: Rose, the daughter of Kristin Davis's Charlotte York, is a teenager now. And of course she decides that she's not the biological girl she was born as but is actually a boy and wants to be called Rock instead.

Kim Catrall was smart enough not to come back for this train wreck, save for one cameo. As for Carrie Bradshaw, her husband, Mr. Big (Chris Noth), was killed off during the first episode while riding a Peloton, allowing Carrie to eventually jump back into the dating pool again in an effort to make the character somewhat interesting. But watching a fiftysomething Carrie navigate single life is awkward and forced, to put it mildly.

Thankfully, a solid majority of Americans were as nauseated as my wife and I were by watching this once-great franchise become reduced to an MSNBC/DNC-approved dumpster fire. On Rotten Tomatoes, the audience score is just 33 percent approval for *And Just Like That*, 47 percentage points below the original *Sex and the City*'s 80 percent audience approval rating.

Still, nothing is safe, thanks to the geniuses that run HBO. Check out what it had to say when *Gone with the Wind*, the highest-grossing film in US history for twenty-five years, was pulled from its film library.

"These racist depictions were wrong then and are wrong today," HBO Max said in a statement. "[Keeping] this title up without an explanation and a denouncement of those depictions would be irresponsible."

Gone with the Wind only won eight Oscars. But today it would be disqualified from competition for accurately portraying life during the Civil War in the Deep South.

As for the 2024 Oscars' mandate on diversity and inclusion, the Academy can breathe a sigh of relief that the *New York Times* has its back:

"The Oscars' New Diversity Rules Are Sweeping but Safe," reads the thumbs-up headline after the changes were announced.

Yes. Safe. That's totally what the art of moviemaking will continue to be: safe.

They make *me* want to vomit . . . as do many Democrats today who seem to be openly embracing anti-Semitism, especially after the worst attack on Jews in more than eight decades.

CHAPTER 15

The Democrats' Jewish Problem

Democrats were positively outraged over Robert F. Kennedy Jr.'s remarks that COVID-19 was a man-made biological weapon.

"COVID-19, there's an argument that it is ethnically targeted," Kennedy said at a dinner in New York City in a video obtained by the *New York Post*. "COVID-19 is targeted to attack Caucasians and Black people. The people that are most immune are Ashkenazi Jews and Chinese."

Kennedy later clarified that his comments were misinterpreted and said he was simply citing a 2021 NIH study on the matter, but the damage was done.

New York Times: *"Robert F. Kennedy Jr. Airs Bigoted New Covid Conspiracy Theory about Jews and Chinese"*

Newsweek: *"Robert Kennedy Jr. Called Out by His Sister for 'Deplorable' Remarks"*

Politico: *"White House Calls Antisemitic Covid Conspiracy Theory Voiced by RFK Jr. 'Vile'"*

OK, but what was the reaction after Rep. Pramila Jayapal (D-WA) called one of our closest allies, Israel, "a racist state" as Israeli president

Isaac Herzog was arriving in Washington, DC? How did the same *New York Times*, for example, which called RFK Jr.'s comments bigoted, react to Jayapal in its op-ed pages? "The Hysterical Overreaction to Jayapal's 'Racist State' Gaffe."

And *Newsweek*? "Rep. Jayapal Was Right: Israel Is a Racist State."

How about *Politico*? "Congressional Progressive Caucus Chair Walks Back Comment on Israel Being 'Racist.'"

A few things to unpack here: for starters, the *New York Times* piece calling the reaction to Jayapal's so-called gaffe a "hysterical overreaction" was written by Michelle Goldberg, who also authored this piece for the *Times* in 2022: "Anti Semitism Increased under Trump. Then It Got Even Worse."

You can't make this stuff up, folks. And it gets even better over at the *Daily Beast*, which somehow blamed (checks notes) Republicans for having the audacity to condemn Jayapal's "misstep": "GOP Seizes on Pramila Jayapal's Israel Misstep to Split Democrats."

"When Progressive Caucus Chairwoman Rep. Pramila Jayapal (D-WA) called Israel 'a racist state,' she was quick to apologize and walk back her comment," the story somehow not labeled an opinion piece reads. "But Republicans weren't going to just let a good controversy die."

But Jayapal's comment onstage during a Netroots Nation conference wasn't just a manner of misspeaking. She clearly meant it. And we know this because Jayapal, a member of the Squad, didn't attend Israeli president Herzog's address to Congress in 2023, laughably pointing to a scheduling conflict.

Speaking of the Squad, there is a pattern of anti-Semitic remarks clearly unfolding over the years. Take Rep. Ilhan Omar (D-MN), who once declared that "Israel has hypnotized the world," as an example. "May Allah awaken the people and help them see the evil doings of Israel," she added.

Omar also suggested that Jewish people are buying political support through bribery. "It's all about the Benjamins baby," she tweeted to her nearly three million followers back in 2019.

All told, nine House Democrats voted against a 2023 resolution brought to the floor declaring that Israel is *not* a racist state: Ilhan Omar, Alexandria Ocasio-Cortez, Jamaal Bowman, Summer Lee, Cori Bush, André Carson, Delia Ramirez, Ayanna Pressley, and Rashida Tlaib, who again accused Israel of practicing apartheid, which she has stated multiple times in the past.

So, did the *New York Times* condemn Tlaib for repeating such an outlandish remark? Nope. Instead, here's their most recent profile on the Michigan Squad member from earlier this year, titled "What Rashida Tlaib Represents":

"Tlaib has been criticized, sometimes viciously, by Republicans and pro-Israel Democrats for calling Israel an 'apartheid regime,' and for her support of the Boycott, Divestment and Sanctions movement, which aims to end military occupation by exerting economic pressure on Israel," reads the profile, which couldn't have been written better by the congresswoman's PR shop if it tried. And the portrayal of Tlaib as a victim of "vicious" attacks after making such comments is truly something to behold.

As for AOC, she perfectly encapsulates the double standard here. On one hand, she stated at the time that RFK Jr. has "trafficked in antisemitism." So if that's the case, surely she would condemn Jayapal for her outlandish comments about Israel, right? Of course not. Instead, AOC stayed silent and even openly embraced Jayapal on the House floor as a show of solidarity as the controversy was blowing up.

This Gallup poll from 2023 is galling: When Democrat voters were asked about who they sympathized with most in the Middle East, 49 percent said Palestine, while just 38 percent said Israel.

During an explosive July 2023 Select Subcommittee on the Weaponization of the Federal Government hearing on Capitol Hill, RFK Jr. was a target of his own party once again.

Before the hearing, 102 Democrats signed a letter saying he should not be afforded the platform to speak and accusing him of being an anti-Semite. Even some members of Kennedy's own family denounced the remarks, while White House press secretary Karine Jean-Pierre called the comments "vile," adding that they put American lives in danger.

What wasn't funny was Rashida Tlaib's reaction to the unthinkable, horrific pure evil that Hamas inflicted on innocent Israelis in October 2023, when whole families, including children and babies, were executed by these terrorist animals, and grandmothers were murdered in their own beds: the congresswoman first decided to put a Palestinian flag outside of her office, along with an LGBTQ+ flag. Gee, I wonder what would happen if Hamas ever encountered someone in Gaza with an LGBTQ+ flag outside their home? Perhaps only being stoned to death would be considered a mercy killing.

But then a truly telling and horrifying thing happened: Tlaib was in the halls of Congress after hours when the intrepid Hillary Vaughn of Fox News began peppering her with very fair questions.

"Congresswoman, Hamas terrorists have cut off babies' heads and burned children alive. Do you support Israel's rights to defend themselves against this brutality?"

Tlaib said *nothing*. I mean, really . . . how hard would it have been to condemn such an act?

"You can't comment about Hamas terrorists chopping off babies' heads?" Vaughn pressed. "Congresswoman, do you have a comment on Hamas terrorists chopping off babies' heads? You have nothing to say about Hamas terrorists chopping off babies' heads?"

Tlaib hurried away, escaping on an elevator. Again, this is a sitting member of the US Congress who once openly cried next to AOC on the House floor in 2019 over kids in cages at the southern US border under Trump.

Meanwhile, RFK Jr. took offense to his fellow Democrats attempting to prevent him from speaking on Capitol Hill while giving a full-throated defense of the First Amendment.

"This itself is evidence of the problem that this hearing was convened to address. This is an attempt to censor a censorship hearing," Kennedy said, holding up the letter calling for his testimony to be repressed.

"Censorship is antithetical to our party," he added. "It was appalling to my father [former attorney general Robert F. Kennedy], my uncle [former president John F. Kennedy], FDR [former president Franklin Delano Roosevelt], [former president] Harry Truman to [former president] Thomas Jefferson.

"I know many of the people who wrote this letter. I don't believe there's a single person who signed this letter who believes I'm antisemitic."

Democrats did nothing when it came to leveling any punishment against Pramila Jayapal after she accused Israel of being racist. They also said nothing about Tlaib staying silent on decapitated babies in Israel. But they were positively apocalyptic after Joe Biden's primary challenger said what he said.

It's called selective outrage. And it's beyond phony.

Almost no tests at Harvard University are what anyone would deem as easy. But when it came to the easiest one of all, Harvard flunked in spectacular fashion in late 2023.

Remember Claudine Gay? She's now the former president of Harvard, because the university decided to fire her after overwhelming pressure following revelations that she had plagiarized on at least forty occasions in the past. But that shouldn't have been the reason for her dismissal. Instead, she should have been ousted for defending the right of anti-Israel protesters to call for the genocide of Jews on campus.

And she did so under oath on Capitol Hill no less.

"At Harvard, does calling for the genocide of Jews violate Harvard's rules of bullying and harassment?" Rep. Elise Stefanik (R-NY) asked in a House hearing on anti-Semitism on campus in December 2023.

"It can be, depending on the context," Gay replied before being pressed on exactly what that context might be.

"When it crosses into conduct," she said. This answer resulted in extensive blowback on social media, along with the hashtag #HamasUniversity and calls for Gay to be fired.

Gee. I wonder what "context" Gay would apply to calls on her campus for the genocide of Blacks or those among the LGBTQ+ community, and if that kind of rhetoric is just fine up until the point someone gets hospitalized or murdered. But Harvard wouldn't budge because Gay was a DEI (Diversity, Equity, Inclusion) hire, and they feared backlash from the left.

"As members of the Harvard Corporation, we today reaffirm our support for President Gay's continued leadership of Harvard University. Our extensive deliberations affirm our confidence that President Gay is the right leader to help our community heal and to address the very serious societal issues we are facing," Harvard's governing body said in a statement.

Yes, nothing says unity quite like Jewish students fearing for their lives on campus.

"Multiple times a week on my way to class, I walk by mobs of people chanting 'from the river to the sea.' . . . I talk to my Jewish friends on campus every day. They tell me how afraid they are to go to class," shared Harvard student Jonathan Frieden during a press conference on Capitol Hill following Gay's testimony.

Overall, according to a 2023 survey by the Anti-Defamation League (ADL), nearly three-quarters of Jewish college students in the United States have experienced or witnessed anti-Semitism on their campuses since the start of the school year. And at last check, more than fourteen hundred people were massacred in Israel in October 2023 in the worst attack on Jews since the Holocaust. But instead of the country uniting behind the Jewish people, hatred of the Jewish community here in the United States only intensified. And that hatred came primarily from the far left.

"There is only one solution: Intifada revolution," pro-Palestinian students chanted at Harvard and other schools recently. An intifada is a call for violence against Israel.

As far as this BS that Harvard is a champion of free speech, it should be noted that the university finished last in the 2024 College Free Speech Rankings, per a survey of more than 55,000 students at

248 schools by the Foundation for Individual Rights and Expression (FIRE).

Harvard's final score among those 248 schools? Zero. Point. Zero. On a 100-point scale.

Why is that? Well, when thirty-four Harvard student groups signed a statement declaring that they "hold the Israeli regime entirely responsible for all unfolding violence" after October 7, 2023, and Gay remained silent for days, that was bad enough. But things were different in 2017, however, when Gay and Harvard withdrew ten acceptances to incoming freshmen over some memes shared during *a private chat* online. So much for free speech. . . .

"The Admissions Committee was disappointed to learn that several students in a private group chat for the Class of 2021 were sending messages that contained offensive messages and graphics," read a copy of the Admissions Office's email to those students obtained by Harvard's student newspaper, the *Crimson*. "As we understand you were among the members contributing such material to this chat, we are asking that you submit a statement by tomorrow at noon to explain your contributions and actions for discussion with the Admissions Committee."

Harvard, however, didn't demand a statement from those thirty-four Harvard student groups explaining their contributions and actions in defending the Hamas attacks while blaming the "apartheid regime" for being attacked on October 7.

And how's this for the stat to end all stats: the *Crimson* surveyed professors on campus as far as what ideology they would deem themselves to be. Get this: 97 percent answered either somewhat liberal or very liberal, while only 2 percent deemed themselves conservatives.

Gay was compelled to step down, yes, but she's still a professor there and earns nearly $900,000 per year (no, really). So these university presidents can be removed, but there is a cancer still there on many campuses. A cancer that basically allows only opinions from one ideological side. Change the hiring practices, change the culture. But that ain't going to happen.

So much for the most important diversity of all: the diversity of thoughts and ideas. And some prominent faculty members have seen and heard enough.

"The system at Harvard along with the ideology that grips far too many of the students and faculty, the ideology that works only along axes of oppression and places Jews as oppressors and therefore intrinsically evil, is itself evil," announced Rabbi David Wolpe, a visiting scholar at Harvard Divinity School, following Gay's testimony.

"Ignoring Jewish suffering is evil. Belittling or denying the Jewish experience, including unspeakable atrocities, is a vast and continuing catastrophe," he added. Now for the most disturbing part: a December 2023 survey conducted by the Harvard CAPS/Harris Poll found that 51 percent of Americans between the ages of eighteen and twenty-four said they believed the "long-term answer" to the Israel-Palestinian war was for "Israel to be ended and given to Hamas and the Palestinians."

You have to be effing kidding me.

As for Joe Biden, here's the one part of the book where I'll give him some credit: he was steadfast in his support of Israel on the day of the attack and every day afterward. He has paid a considerable price for it in states like Michigan that he must win to gain reelection, where one in-state poll by Lake Research Partners showed Biden's approval entering 2024 among Muslim and Arab Democrat voters there falling to 16 percent. Biden still is Biden, of course, so as his polling plummeted among Muslim and young voters, he tempered his vocal support for Israel and then some because there was an election to be won, and that can't happen without Michigan.

The Squad is one of the highest-profile factions in the Democratic Party. Media coverage has been as favorable as it gets since they came into existence following the 2018 midterms. But Democrats have shown a strange tolerance for its members saying blatantly anti-Semitic things.

But perhaps, finally, the media is beginning to notice the sentiment that has been spewed for some time now.

"These last few days have been a real eye-opening period for a lot of people—a lot of Democrats, a lot of progressives—in terms of anti-semitism on the left," CNN's Jake Tapper said after the Hamas terror attacks on Israel.

The last few days?

To quote Detective John McClane, "Welcome to the party, pal!"

So the next time you hear any Dems evoke something clearly anti-Semitic or accuse someone of being an anti-Semite, just remember the tolerance they continue to show when members of their own party repeatedly engage in the same rhetoric.

Speaking of making excuses, let me tell you about the time when cocaine was found near the Situation Room in the White House and not one clue could be uncovered in the most surveilled property in the world as to who it could possibly belong to.

Some Dems, including Senator Joe Biden and President Clinton, once made fighting crime a top priority and championed the 1994 crime bill. Sadly, those donkeys have long been put out to pasture.

PART IV

Remember When Democrats Cared about Law and Order?

Cocaine found in the West Wing near the Situation Room, and hardly anyone investigating the crime seems to care very much.

Death and destruction—not in a war zone in eastern Ukraine, but the South Side of Chicago. And hardly anyone in legacy media, at least on a national level, seems to care very much.

The southern US border is wide open, with terrorists and fentanyl pouring in, yet Team Biden doesn't seem to care very much. In fact, when Texas took matters into its own hands and installed barbed wire where illegals were pouring over, the Biden administration went to the Supreme Court to order them to stop. Whose side are they on, anyway?

Believe it or not, there was a time Democrats actually cared about law and order. Barack Obama was decried by the left as the Deporter in Chief, for goodness' sake. Joe Biden led the charge for the tough 1994 crime bill. Bill Clinton supported the death penalty, as did JFK. Lyndon B. Johnson literally declared a war on crime. Bobby Kennedy declared a war on gangs as attorney general.

Those days are long gone. We're "reimagining" police forces now while Democrat mayors are cutting funding where it's needed most in law enforcement. Idiots in the media on channels like CNN and MSNBC went on the air in the summer of 2020 and defended rioters and antifa while downplaying little things like firebombing federal buildings in Portland and running the police out of their own head-quarters in Seattle.

Who could have possibly left a bag of nose candy next to the Situation Room? We may never find out, thanks to a swamp that seemingly made sure the culprit was never revealed.

CHAPTER 16

Cocainegate—and Why No One Trusts Our Institutions Anymore

July 2, 2023: A powdery substance is found near the West Executive entrance in the White House, which is located adjacent to the Situation Room.

Quickly, the Secret Service confirms the substance is cocaine.

An easy case to solve? Well, this *is* 1600 Pennsylvania Ave., one of the most surveilled properties in the world, so solving this mystery should be a relatively painless process: Just rewind the video from one of the many cameras mounted in such a sensitive area, and the culprit should be easy to identify. There's probably also fingerprints or DNA on the dime bag, another slam dunk.

But just eleven days later, the Secret Service declares that the case is closed, citing a lack of physical evidence such as fingerprints or DNA. As for all of those video cameras, they turned out to be as useless as the ones filming Jeffrey Epstein's prison cell when he (cough) committed suicide.

"There was no surveillance video footage found that provided investigative leads or any other means for investigators to identify who may have deposited the found substance in this area," the agency said in a statement in mid-July.

"The FBI's laboratory results . . . did not develop latent fingerprints and insufficient DNA was present for investigative comparisons. Therefore, the Secret Service is not able to compare evidence against the known pool of individuals," the statement added.

Say what?

Of course, most of the media decided that this was a perfectly normal explanation and didn't bother asking questions such as . . .

Is the agency saying that whoever the owner of the cocaine was somehow had the wherewithal to wipe down the bag to erase fingerprints before leaving it behind?

Was the suspect wearing gloves? If so, it's a bit warm to be doing that in July.

Why weren't all of the members of Biden's White House staff and the First Family drug-tested after the substance was discovered?

And how exactly is there no video footage of said suspect leaving the bag in question? Because one would think there isn't one inch of the White House that is somehow hidden from these cameras.

"The cubbies where the small bag of cocaine was found is a blind spot for surveillance cameras, according to a source familiar with the investigation," read a CNN report.

Well, that's that, I guess. Last one out, shut out the lights. GOP lawmakers, thankfully, were having none of it.

"Every time there's something strange going on with President Biden or his family, or anything regarding his administration or the White House, no one can ever seem to find an answer," Rep. Nancy Mace (R-SC) said. "This is one of the most secure locations in the world, some of the best law enforcement officers in the world, and they don't have any answers."

Rep. Tim Burchett (R-TN) was even more direct.

"Y'all know you can't go into [the White House] without giving your Social Security number anyway, and to say that it's just some weekend visitor, that's bogus," Burchett noted in disputing the explanation provided. "Nobody's buying that at all."

And then there was this from the great Sen. John Kennedy (R-LA).

"Look, I've been in the Situation Room. There are cameras everywhere. I'm pretty sure the Secret Service knows. I don't know who did it. I don't know whose blow it was," he told Fox News before leveling the usual rhetorical dagger. "I probably shouldn't say this, but if my record was as bad as this White House's record, I'd probably give my staff blow too."

Damn, he's good.

Even the White House's effort to spin this tale went off sideways. Earlier that week, after the nose candy was found, White House press secretary Karine Jean-Pierre openly lied, snapping at a *New York Post* reporter who asked if the White House could say "once and for all" that the coke didn't come from a member of the Biden family, "They [the Biden family] were not here on Friday, Saturday, Sunday, or Monday, so to ask that question is incredibly irresponsible! And I'll just leave it there," she scolded.

Except . . . the Biden family, including Hunter Biden, a former cocaine addict, *were* all at the White House until *Friday night*, per a press pool report. Unfortunately, but not surprisingly, no reporters in the White House press corps bothered to reengage and challenge KJP on that simple factoid because by the time Biden's weekend away was over, the news cycle seemingly moved on.

Ultimately, we'll never know who the coke belonged to (I could wager the kids' college funds on someone with the initials HB, but FanDuel or DraftKings would never take that bet). And that's truly disturbing, considering this substance could have been deadly anthrax or ricin in close proximity to the president. As you may have heard, the Oval Office is directly above the Situation Room for a reason.

Ask yourself this: If this had been anthrax, does anyone really think the Secret Service would simply throw their hands up less than two weeks after it was found and say, "Oh, well. We tried"? Of course not. And foreign adversaries such as Russia, China, Iran, and al-Qaeda 2.0

almost certainly watched this story unfold with no consequences to anyone and concluded that it's actually quite easy to penetrate what is supposed to be one of the most secure buildings in the world.

In a related story, trust in institutions is currently at an all-time low in this country, and understandably so. Here's a few reasons why:

We heard for years from Democratic lawmakers, without proof, that then president Trump was actually a Putin stooge and agent of the Kremlin. Many in the partisan press dutifully pushed this dossier-fueled narrative (and still do) despite the fact that Special Counsel Robert Mueller's investigation concluded that these wild claims were untrue.

We saw that the Dobbs decision on abortion was leaked out of the Supreme Court in 2022, and the media cheered the unprecedented breach along with the protests in front of the justices' homes. One man was even arrested for *the attempted murder of Justice Kavanaugh* not long after. And to this day, that mystery of who leaked it, obviously to rally Democrats in a midterm election year, remains unsolved. The investigation somehow came up empty.

Americans living in once-great cities, from New York to Chicago to San Francisco, see their respective Soros-backed attorneys general embrace cashless bail laws that allow criminals to be back out on the street after being arrested in the time it takes to deliver a pizza. Government is supposed to protect its citizens first and foremost. Instead, it's almost as if they're working against that goal.

Donald Trump won the 2016 election. A solid majority of Democratic voters believe the Russians tampered with vote tallies to steal the election from Hillary Clinton. Joe Biden won the 2020 election. An even bigger majority of Republican voters say that the election was stolen from Trump. Result: trust in institutions has so greatly diminished that a whole book could be filled quite easily.

According to Gallup, the American people's confidence in their national institutions is at an all-time low, averaging *just 27 percent*. Context: in the post-Watergate and post-Vietnam era back in 1979, that confidence number was *still* close to 50 percent, despite multiple assassinations of the biggest public figures in the country (JFK, RFK, Martin Luther King Jr.), a seemingly pointless war in Vietnam that cost nearly sixty thousand American lives, and the first US president to resign in office (Nixon).

The country was a complete mess in the late 1970s, yet almost half of its citizens still trusted its government. Today, it's only half that number.

More numbers, per Gallup:

» Just 26 percent have confidence in the public school system.
» Just 23 percent have confidence in the presidency.
» Just 14 percent have confidence in the criminal justice system.
» Just 11 percent have confidence in television news.
» Just 7 percent have trust in Congress. Gas station sushi polls higher.

The Secret Service was created to protect the president and his family. Fortunately for them, it was just cocaine that was found, and not something far, far worse.

And the fact that they couldn't stop this substance from entering the White House, nor could they solve this case, well . . . that should be alarming to Americans already skeptical of the way things work in Washington.

As for our media, assuming the coke belonged to someone in the president's inner circle is just another crazy conspiracy theory, like Covid coming from a lab or social media censoring conservatives.

Washington Post: *"Cocaine Was Found at the White House. It Wasn't the First Time"*

The **New Republic**: *"Conservatives' White House Cocaine Theories Are Getting More Absurd by the Day"*

Newsweek: *"Trump Floats Flurry of Theories on Cocaine Found at White House"*

The **Daily Beast**: *"Tasteless: Republicans Continue to Blame Hunter Biden for White House Cocaine Saga"*

Cocaine was left at the White House near the Situation Room. The Secret Service wrapped up its investigation without interviewing one member of the Biden family. No drug tests were administered. No video could be found. No fingerprints on the bag.

The American public watched all of this unfold. They've also watched indictment after indictment be leveled against a former president who happens to be the biggest threat not just to the current party in power but to the current establishment of government institutions as a whole.

It's tragic to see trust in leadership fall this far, this fast. And it's not just in the federal government but in city governments in places like Chicago, a once-great city that is practically unrecognizable from its heyday. There's a big reason for that. . . .

CHAPTER 17

Chicago: Not My Kind
of Town Anymore

Richard J. Daley was Chicago's mayor in 1964, earning term after term between 1955 and 1976. Daley was a Democrat but would never be confused with Chicago's current mayor, Brandon Johnson, elected in 2023, who takes the "Let's Go" out of "Let's Go Brandon." But more on him in a bit.

The Daley name is arguably the most consequential in Chicago politics in the modern era. Richard J. Daley was in office for twenty-one years, from the the mid-1950s to the mid-1970s. His son, Richard M. Daley, was mayor for twenty-two years, from 1989 to 2011.

You can agree or disagree with Daley on a range of issues, but the numbers are the numbers. The year Daley took office, there were 854 murders in the city. By the end of his tenure in 2009, the number had dropped almost by half, to 431.

But when Lori Lightfoot was elected in 2019, those gains were almost entirely erased. Murders in 2020: 772. Murders in 2021: 796. Murders in 2022: 695.

The current mayor, Brandon Johnson, has supported defunding the police, for example. His own words in 2020 here:

"People are not feeling any safer, communities have not transformed by putting more money into the police," Johnson told WBEZ's *Reset* in 2020. "I'm absolutely confident that we will be the generation that responds and reacts to the global movement that is calling for redirecting money away from policing and militarizing police forces and directing dollars into job opportunities, transportation, health care and housing for people."

The same year, Johnson backed this sentiment up by introducing a nonbinding resolution on the Cook County Board that called for reallocating funds from police to social services. But during his run for mayor, suddenly that rhetoric went away. Go figure.

The year is 2023. Mayor Lori Lightfoot is running for reelection. On paper, it looks like a piece of cake. After all, Lightfoot won with nearly *74 percent* of the vote in 2019.

But crime is getting more out of control than usual. A WBEZ poll heading into 2023 shows that nearly two-thirds of Chicagoans say they don't feel safe. After all, they're living in a city that recently experienced one of the worst hate crimes in recent history, maybe ever. . . .

In January 2019, two men attacked poor Jussie Smollett at 2:00 a.m. after the actor had a hankering for a Subway sandwich during the coldest night of the year. And lo and behold, these MAGA goons were not only waiting, they absolutely were prepared . . . right down to having a noose and bleach at the ready just in case any Black, gay, Democrat-supporting actors just happened to be walking around at that time on a weekday night in subzero weather.

"This is MAGA country!" the alleged assailants shouted at Smollett.

Ummm . . . wait. No it ain't!

You all know what happened from there: Police quickly realized Smollett was lying. The MAGA attackers were actually two Nigerian guys (I met them in a greenroom at Fox once, and they're absolutely hilarious) whom Smollett had hired and was even smart enough to pay with a personal check.

Most of the national media looked more foolish than usual in peddling this horseshit seemingly without the kind of skepticism this kind of story warranted, given just how perfect this "crime" was, almost like it was straight out of a bad movie. Smollett was arrested for lying to police on five felony disorderly conduct charges.

And then a funny thing happened: Cook County's prosecutor, Kim Foxx, dropped all the charges.

"Yes, falsely reporting a hate crime makes me angry, and anyone who does that deserves the community's outrage," Foxx said in March 2019. "But, as I've said since before I was elected, we must separate the people at whom we are angry from the people of whom we are afraid."

No . . . reporting a false crime shouldn't just make a prosecutor angry. It should, given the overwhelming evidence, compel them to punish the person who wasted countless hours of police investigators' time when they could have been investigating *actual crimes*.

Wanna know why the crime crisis never seems to get better these days? Because of prosecutors like Foxx and mayors like Brandon Johnson. Think about this one-two punch: The nation's third-largest city has a mayor who believes in a "more comprehensive approach," and that more social services are the answer. And when the police who are left do arrest someone, those crimes aren't prosecuted in many cases because officials like Kim Foxx believe "we must separate the people at whom we are angry with from the people of whom we are afraid."

In her first three years alone, Foxx dismissed more than twenty-five thousand felony cases—including some involving charges of murder and other violent crimes—per a *Chicago Tribune* report. Overall, Foxx has dropped 35 percent more charges than did her predecessor.

In the 2023 mayoral election, Lightfoot would go on to lose in a runoff, capturing just 16.8 percent of the vote. Johnson defeated Democratic moderate Paul Vallas by a slim margin a few weeks later, but here's the utterly maddening part: approximately 560,000 votes were cast in this all-important election in a city of 2.15 million residents eligible to vote.

So, who's to blame for the current state of Chicago? It would be easy to look no further than the 70 percent of voters who couldn't be bothered to go to the polls. But the fact that so many citizens are checked out of the political process probably means Chicago's politicians have failed so much, nobody really trusts that they'll change anything.

The crime crisis has resulted in a record number of people and businesses leaving the city. The education system is a shambles. Just how bad is it? Nearly 80 percent of Chicago public school students *can't read at grade-level requirements*, while only 15 percent meet proficiency standards in math. Throw in some of the highest taxes in the country (and my Bears becoming one of the worst teams in the league), and suddenly Chicago isn't anyone's kind of town anymore. And in a related story, Mayor Johnson's approval rating dropped to 28 percent just months after he was elected.

That last number shows a decrease when compared to two horrific years, so on cue, the usual suspects in the media point to it to say how much things are improving in Chicago.

The same trick is done with inflation. Instead of comparing the number to the 1.4 percent it was when Trump left office, the media largely takes what inflation eventually climbed to under Biden (9.1 percent) and portrays it as low by doing a comparison to the high point instead of the low point (1.4 percent) during the Trump administration.

Kim Foxx is also somehow still serving as Cook County prosecutor. And when she runs for reelection, I'd put money on the chances that she'll get another four years. Because, until sane and sober people get sick and tired enough of living scared while their children are barely getting an education, it's lather, rinse, repeat in places like Chicago.

Hollywood doesn't have much to say about what's happening there. But there are exceptions, like the great Denzel Washington, the star of modern classics *Crimson Tide, Inside Man, Glory, Remember the Titans*, and my personal favorite, 2001's *Training Day* (Denzel plays a top-ten all-time bad guy, if you haven't seen it).

"It starts in the home," Washington said of rampant violence in Chicago. "If the father is not in the home, the boy will find a father in the streets. I saw it in my generation and every generation before me, and every one ever since. If the streets raise you, then the judge becomes your mother and prison becomes your home."

And he's correct. According to Fathers.com, "Children from father-less homes are more likely to be poor, become involved in drug and alcohol abuse, drop out of school, and suffer from health and emotional problems. Boys are more likely to become involved in crime, and girls are more likely to become pregnant as teens."

Vice President Dan Quayle once made the same obvious point and was pilloried by Democrats, Hollywood, and the media for pointing out the problem with single motherhood as it relates to the plight of children without a father in the home.

"Bearing babies irresponsibly is, simply, wrong. Failing to support children one has fathered is wrong. We must be unequivocal about this. It doesn't help matters when prime-time TV has Murphy Brown—a character who supposedly epitomizes today's intelligent, highly paid professional woman—mocking the importance of fathers by bearing a child alone and calling it just another 'life-style choice,'" Quayle said all the way back in 1992.

The New York *Daily News*, as much a rag as anything that exists in "journalism," went with this headline following Quayle's speech: "Quayle to Murphy Brown: You Tramp!"

No. That's not what he said. Not even remotely close. But no matter: Candice Bergen, who played Murphy Brown on CBS, won an Emmy Award that year for lines like this:

"I couldn't possibly do a worse job raising my kid alone than the Reagans did with theirs."

Bergen and the show's writers would go on to milk the controversy in profoundly dishonest fashion, saying time and again that Quayle was not promoting two-parent households but attacking single mothers.

"Last night, they said I attacked single mothers. That's a lie. . . . Winning an Emmy is not a license to lie," Quayle responded.

In retrospect, who was right? The numbers tell the story:

In 1980, the number of children born outside of marriage was 18.4 percent.

In 1992, at the time of Quayle's comments, the number of children born outside marriage had risen to 30 percent.

In 2009, that number had risen to 41 percent. And in that same year, for women under age thirty, a majority of babies were born outside of marriage.*

So what are the consequences of all of this? According to the National Assessment of Adult Literacy, "Two-thirds of students who cannot read proficiently by the end of the fourth grade will end up in jail or on welfare."

Quayle *was* right. Just ask, well . . . Candice Bergen. Here she is ten years later after the controversy in 2002:

"I never have really said much about the whole episode, which was endless. But his speech was a perfectly intelligent speech about fathers not being dispensable and nobody agreed with that more than I did."

You have to be effing kidding me, Candice.

So how bad were things in the Windy City in 2023?

Well, a prominent community group called Native Sons is requesting Chicago's gangs to stop doing the gunfight thing during daytime hours between 9:00 a.m. and 9:00 p.m.

"We have to start somewhere," Native Sons cofounder Tatiana Atkins told CWB Chicago. "Our goal is to approach our city's gun violence problem strategically and not all at once. Things didn't become this way overnight, and change won't happen overnight."

The ordinance has been advocated by Chicago City Council member Maria Hadden, who describes herself as the first "Black, queer woman" to serve on the council.

To quote Dark Helmet in Mel Brooks's *Spaceballs*, "How many ass-

---

* "Percentage of Births to Unmarried Women in the United States from 1980 to 2021," Statistica, https://www.statista.com/statistics/276025/us-percentage-of-births-to-unmarried-women/.

holes do we got on this ship anyway?" I mean, can you imagine this conversation:

Gang member #1: *"Hey, who's up for a drive-by shooting at the White Sox game tonight?"*

Gang member #2: *"Sounds great! But wait a minute, what time is it?"*

Gang member #3: *"It's 7:00 p.m. Let's grab some dinner first."*

Gang member #1: *"Why?"*

Gang member #2: *"Because haven't you heard? City Council just passed a law that says we can't murder anyone between the hours of 9:00 a.m. and 9:00 p.m."*

Gang member #3: *"That sucks, man. I might not be in the mood in two hours."*

Gang member #2: *"Rules are rules. Do you know what kind of trouble we can get in if we start executing people during the day?"*

Gang member #1: *Good point. Hey! Who's up for some flapjacks instead? Too early for flapjacks?"*

You get the point. Gun-free zones don't work. And telling gang members when they can and cannot kill people isn't going to work.

Speaking of the White Sox, did you hear what happened on August 26, 2023?

The Sox, having a disappointing year after a surprising success in 2022, were home to the putrid Oakland (likely soon to be Las Vegas) A's for a Saturday-night game on a nice summer evening on the city's South Side. Twenty-one thousand people were in attendance.

And then two women were shot *inside* the ballpark. One in the leg. The other in the stomach. Both fortunately survived.

But here's where things go completely nuts: neither team officials nor the police decided to stop the game. Play ball! Even when fans get shot.

"Upon receiving notification of this incident, CPD responded immediately and deployed additional resources while coordinating with White Sox security to maintain the safety of those who were in attendance or working at the game," police said in the statement. "At no time was it believed there was an active threat."

No active threat? How could *anyone* possibly confirm this?

A postgame concert featuring (checks notes) Vanilla Ice, Rob Base, and Tone Loc was canceled, however. Why? To allow authorities to investigate the shooting hours later, when it was determined the shots fired *did* occur inside the ballpark.

But no worries, Mayor Brandon Johnson has everything under control, because in August 2023 he filed a lawsuit against two automakers (Kia and Hyundai) for lacking appropriate anti-theft measures, which, Johnson concludes, is fueling rising car thefts.

No, really . . .

"The impact of car theft on Chicago residents can be deeply destabilizing, particularly for low- to middle-income workers who have fewer options for getting to work and taking care of their families," Johnson said in announcing the lawsuit. "The failure of Kia and Hyundai to install basic auto-theft prevention technology in these models is sheer negligence, and as a result, a citywide and nationwide crime spree around automobile theft has been unfolding right before our eyes."

Yep. This moron is blaming the carmakers, not the people, you know, *stealing the cars* or the district attorney who allows these criminals back out onto the street.

Overall, between May 2022 and May 2023, according to Chicago's ABC affiliate, more than twenty thousand cars have been stolen, a

73 percent increase when compared to the average the previous three years.

Some Democrats actually used to be tough on crime, including Bill and Hillary Clinton . . . at least the 1990s versions of themselves. Here's Hillary at Keene State College in 1996. Close your eyes hard enough, and it might as well be Dirty Harry giving this speech:

"They are not just gangs of kids anymore. They are often the kinds of kids that are called 'superpredators.' No conscience, no empathy. We can talk about why they ended up that way, but first we have to bring them to heel," the First Lady reasonably said at the time.

Seriously, what was wrong with that observation? If you can shoot or stab another human being in cold blood and continue to do so without conscience or empathy for the victim or their families, that makes you a superpredator. Period.

But then the woke-mind virus got hold of Hillary when she was running for president in 2016, and suddenly, like a jellyfish without a spine, she spectacularly flip-flopped after being confronted by Black Lives Matter at a campaign event.

"In that speech, I was talking about the impact violent crime and vicious drug cartels were having on communities across the country and the particular danger they posed to children and families," Clinton said in a statement obtained by CBS News. "Looking back, I shouldn't have used those words, and I wouldn't use them today."

Not to be outdone, Bill Clinton has also apologized for (checks notes) enforcing the law.

"We have too many people in prison," he said at one of Hillary's campaign stops in 2015. "And we wound up spending—putting so many people in prison that there wasn't enough money left to educate them, train them for new jobs and increase the chances when they came out that they could live productive lives."

Today's Democrats now hold extreme positions on crime. Take future presidential candidate John Fetterman, for example:

"I was on a panel with Secretary [John] Wetzel, before the pandemic hit, and he said something remarkable that I agree with. He said, 'We could reduce our prison population by a third and not make anyone less safe in Pennsylvania.' And that's a profound statement."

There are currently thirty-seven thousand people in confinement in the state of Pennsylvania. Philadelphia saw more than five hundred murders in 2022, which matches the all-time high set in 1990, and Fetterman wants to release more than twelve thousand prisoners back into the population and thinks no one in the state will be *less safe*?

Citizens feeling safe should be the cornerstone of any republic. Just ask Hillary Clinton in 2016: "I have been for border security for years. I voted for border security in the United States Senate. And my comprehensive immigration reform plan of course includes border security," she said.

But today's donkeys don't like to talk about securing the border at all. This is political suicide, of course, but that's exactly the self-infliction these folks are doing to themselves, right up to the president and vice president.

CHAPTER 18

Democrats Were for Border Security, until They Were against It

The young adult men arrived in the city that never sleeps, traveling by bus to New York's Port Authority. It was their first trip there, and they had traveled from far away.

These weren't spring breakers or tourists, nor were they students. But somehow the trip was entirely paid for without any parental assistance. Instead, it was the US government, and therefore the American taxpayer, footing the bill for these illegal migrants to come to the Big Apple.

In a sane world, these folks wouldn't even be in the country. We would have border security, a border wall, and an orderly system that welcomes those who want to come here legally. But in this insane country, under an equally insane Democratic Party, wall construction gets halted. The Democratic nominee for president at the time implored those from other countries to "immediately surge the border" (yes, that's a quote from candidate Joe Biden). The same president then ended the Remain in Mexico policy crafted by the Trump administration, which was highly effective.

The same president's handlers put *Kamala freaking Harris* in charge of fixing the border crisis, the same person who has said she does not want to treat people coming across the border illegally as criminals, and compared ICE to the KKK. And then Biden's impossibly inept press secretary actually said this without her nose hitting a reporter in the face from it growing so much (emphasis mine):

"The president *inherited a mess* because of what the last administration did. We inherited a mess," the hapless Karine Jean-Pierre dishonestly explained when actually asked about the crisis. "And, you know, Republicans in Congress made it worse by blocking comprehensive immigration reform. And so what you're seeing from this president is he's acting. *He's acting to protect,* to continue to protect the border, *secure the border,* and also deal with irregular migration."

As of September 2023, the final numbers for Fiscal 2023, per the House Committee on Homeland Security, showed that approximately 7.5 million people have entered this country illegally since Biden took office. *Seven-point-five million people.* That's more than the individual populations of thirty-eight states.

To quote Michael Keaton's Bruce Wayne character in *Batman,* "You wanna get nuts? C'mon LET'S GET NUTS!"

Per the *Wall Street Journal* in 2021:

> The Biden administration is in talks to offer immigrant families that were separated during the Trump administration around $450,000 a person in compensation, according to people familiar with the matter, as several agencies work to resolve lawsuits filed on behalf of parents and children who say the government subjected them to lasting psychological trauma.
>
> The U.S. Departments of Justice, Homeland Security, and Health and Human Services are considering payments that could amount to close to $1 million a family, though the final numbers could shift.

Thankfully, after severe blowback, this loco legislation never went through. But subtly, through other means, many illegals are enjoying a good life after breaking into the country. Take those guys mentioned at the beginning of the chapter (the ones on their own version of a fully subsidized spring break for life):

After getting a free bus ride to Manhattan and a free cell phone upon entering the country, they were put up indefinitely at the four-star Row Hotel. And it's not just the hotel room that many of us can't afford after staying a night or two from several hundred dollars per night that they're getting, but also free food, which many proceed to throw out.

Per the *New York Post* in January 2023:

> Disturbing photos show garbage bags full of sandwiches and bagels awaiting disposal at the four-star Row NYC hotel near Times Square, where the city pays a daily rate as high as $500 per room, hotel employee Felipe Rodriguez told the *Post*. Other images show a hotel room littered with empty beer cans and bottles following a wild World Cup viewing party in November.

Overall, according to FAIR (Federation for American Immigration Reform), US taxpayers pay approximately $182 *billion* (that's right, billion with a *b*) annually to cover the cost of illegals in this country. Room and board, meals, cell service. It's the biggest "surge the border" incentive program in the world. Who wouldn't want to come here if this is what's being provided?

There are currently 630,000 homeless people in America. Of that 630,000, more than 67,000 are veterans who served this country, more than 10 percent. How isn't every American, regardless of how they vote, not standing up and screaming about this? A fraction of that $182 billion that's being spent to cover the cost of illegals in this country could house every veteran on the street, but that's where the priorities are for the Democratic Party: it's not only noncitizens over citizens, but foreigners over our own *veterans*.

And why? In the hopes they'll all be able to vote one day, which appears to be the ultimate goal. Just last year, the Washington, DC,

City Council passed a bill that allows noncitizens and illegals to vote in local elections. New York City tried to pass a similar bill that would have allowed eight hundred thousand illegals to vote, but fortunately a sane Staten Island judge shot it down. Rest assured, if Democrats gain back power in the House and a Democrat occupies the White House again, a move will be made to allow illegals to vote under federal law, guaranteeing one-party rule in this country indefinitely.

It wasn't always this way. Not even close. And not that long ago . . .

We simply cannot allow people to pour into the United States undetected, undocumented, unchecked, and circumventing the line of people who are waiting patiently, diligently, and lawfully to become immigrants in this country.

—SENATOR BARACK OBAMA, 2005

Couldn't agree more.

Barack Obama is the president who deported more illegals than any president in history. Whatever happened to not allowing "people to pour into the United States undetected, undocumented, unchecked, and circumventing the line of people who are waiting patiently, diligently, and lawfully to become immigrants in this country"?

How about President Bill Clinton? What was his record on illegal immigration?

Well . . .

"The jobs they hold might otherwise be held by citizens or legal immigrants. The public service they use impose burdens on our taxpayers. That's why [the Clinton administration] has moved aggressively to secure our borders more by hiring a record number of new border guards, by deporting twice as many criminal aliens as ever before, by cracking down on illegal hiring, by barring welfare benefits to illegal aliens," Clinton said in 1995. And, yes, it is hilarious to think about the apocalyptic reaction any Democrat would get today if they used the term *illegal alien*.

DEMOCRATS WERE FOR BORDER SECURITY

"In the budget I will present to you, we will try to do more to speed the deportation of illegal aliens who are arrested for crimes, to better identify illegal aliens in the workplace as recommended by the commission headed by former Congresswoman Barbara Jordan," Clinton continued. "We are a nation of immigrants. But we are also a nation of laws. It is wrong and ultimately self-defeating for a nation of immigrants to permit the kind of abuse of our immigration laws we have seen in recent years, and we must do more to stop it."

Strong words. Common sense. Clinton had held the record for deportations before Obama broke that record.

The hypocrisy truly is endless.

We do need to address the issue of immigration and the challenge we have of undocumented people in our country. We certainly do not want any more coming in.

—REP. NANCY PELOSI, 2008

A wall, in my view, is an immorality. It's the least effective way to protect the border and the most costly. I can't think of any reason why anyone would think it's a good idea—unless this has something to do with something else.

—ALSO NANCY PELOSI, 2019

I voted numerous times when I was a senator to spend money to build a barrier to try to prevent illegal immigrants from coming in. And I do think you have to control your borders.

—HILLARY CLINTON, 2015

Trump is playing to his base—and his base was attracted to him for a number of reasons, one of which was his anti-immigrant rhetoric. And that was exemplified by the wall. So the wall became more of a symbol than a real plan. He has now decided that he has to do whatever he can to get the wall, to satisfy the base. He has gone so far in

that direction that he does things which are truly unimaginably cruel
and unrelated to the outcome.

—ALSO HILLARY CLINTON, 2018

Make unlawful the hiring of undocumented aliens, with enforcement
by the Justice Department against those employers who engage in a "pat-
tern or practice" of such hiring. Penalties would be civil—injunctions
and fines of $1,000 per undocumented alien hired. Criminal penalties
could be imposed by the courts against employers violating injunctions.
Moreover, employers, and others, receiving compensation for knowingly
assisting an undocumented alien obtain or retain a job would also be
subject to criminal penalties.

Increase significantly the enforcement of the Fair Labor Standards
Act and the Federal Farm Labor Contractor Registration Act, targeted
to areas where heavy undocumented alien hirings occur....

Substantially increase resources available to control the Southern
border, and other entry points, in order to prevent illegal immigration.

—PRESIDENT JIMMY CARTER, 1977

I have not discussed the border wall with President Trump, and do
not support him on the issue.

—ALSO JIMMY CARTER, 2019

Illegal immigration is wrong. We must create a system that converts
the flow of primarily low-skilled illegal immigrants into the United
States into a more manageable and controlled flow of legal immi-
grants who can be absorbed by our economy.

—SEN. CHUCK SCHUMER, 2009

The only way we are going to have a great future in America is if
we welcome and embrace immigrants, dreamers, and all of them,
because our ultimate goal is to help the dreamers, but get a path to

citizenship for all 11 million or however many undocumented there are here.

—ALSO SEN. CHUCK SCHUMER, 2022

Folks, I voted for a fence, I voted, unlike most Democrats—and some of you won't like it—I voted for 700 miles of fence. But, let me tell you, we can build a fence 40 stories high—unless you change the dynamic in Mexico and—and you will not like this, and—punish American employers who knowingly violate the law when, in fact, they hire illegals. Unless you do those two things, all the rest is window dressing. Now, I know I'm not supposed to say it that bluntly, but they're the facts, they're the facts. And so everything else we do is in between here. Everything else we do is at the margins. And the reason why I add that parenthetically, why I believe the fence is needed does not have anything to do with immigration as much as drugs. And let me tell you something folks, people are driving across that border with tons, tons, hear me, tons of everything from byproducts for methamphetamine to cocaine to heroin and it's all coming up through corrupt Mexico.

—SEN. JOE BIDEN, 2006

Building a massive wall that spans the entire southern border is not a serious policy solution. It is a waste of money that diverts attention from genuine threats to our homeland security.

—PRESIDENT JOE BIDEN,

on his first day in office, January 2021

Genuine threats like terrorists in record numbers coming over the border, Mr. President? *That* threat?

At least New York City mayor Eric Adams (D) began telling Team Biden that enough is enough in 2023, after he got a small taste of what border towns in Texas and Arizona have been dealing with for years.

Gov. Greg Abbott of Texas, in what was one of the great political moves we've witnessed in modern times, decided to send migrants to so-called sanctuary cities so they can feel what it's like to have thousands upon thousands of illegals dropped into your community without the means to handle the influx. In August 2023, the number of migrants who have come into New York City topped one hundred thousand.

Adams, a former NYPD detective, estimates the price tag for housing, food, transportation, education, and providing free health care for these illegals will be $12 billion over three years. To put that number in perspective, New York City's 2023 budget includes $171 million for homeless services for those legally living in the city. Doing the math, that $12 billion to take care of illegals is *twenty-three times higher* than the city budget for its homeless.

"We need to control the border. We need to call a state of emergency, and we need to properly fund this national crisis. We need help. And it's not going to get any better," Adams said in August 2023. "From this moment on it's downhill. There is no more room. I was at the Roosevelt Hotel on Saturday, and I went there on Sunday. They lined up around the block, hurting the businesses there; this is not going to get better. We put buses there for cooling systems, but it is just not sustainable."

By "lined up around the block," Adams was referring to people sleeping on the street outside the once-famous hotel. I see scenes like this every time I go into midtown Manhattan to go on Fox: There are people setting up their tents with only cardboard and sheets, seemingly on corners everywhere. The city that thrived under Rudolph Giuliani (R) and Michael Bloomberg (R/I/D) not too long ago was unrecognizable.

Of course Adams, being a virtue-signaling, PC Democrat, will not simply declare that New York is no longer a sanctuary city. When it comes to any politician, always judge them by actions and never their words. So when a growing number of New Yorkers begged Adams to turn away these illegals coming in, the mayor just *had* to share how caring he is.

"New Yorkers, please don't turn against each other. That is what the enemy wants," he said. "This city is supposed to be displaying what the God-like spirit is. And it doesn't mean stating that 'We don't want those people.'"

Hey, it's no skin off of Adams's back. He'll just pass those billions in costs along to taxpayers already experiencing the highest tax rates in the country (this side of California) in order to facilitate that "God-like spirit" for illegals. In a related story, Adams announced in late 2023 that his administration was going to cut services to those living in New York legally to take care of those who are not here legally. These cuts included money allocated to education, sanitation, and the NYPD. It's no wonder more people are escaping New York for red southern states at a pace never seen before.*

So how is New York's largest newspaper covering this crisis that's literally right on its doorstep? Enter Mara Gay of the *New York Times* editorial board, who thinks the city should be welcoming *more* illegals (whom she incorrectly and intentionally dubs "asylum seekers"), regardless of cost or space or quality of life or the negative impact on businesses:

"There is something particularly disappointing about New York City's official response to the asylum seekers, unfolding under the gaze of the Statue of Liberty in the harbor. Nearly four in 10 city residents were born outside the United States. Waves of immigrants—Dutch, Irish, Italian, Jewish, Chinese, Latino and Afro-Caribbean immigrants, along with many others—helped build this city. So did millions of Black Americans who chased dreams in the city after fleeing the tyranny of the Jim Crow South."

Hey, Mara—maybe evoking the Statue of Liberty is more than misleading here, since people came to Ellis Island, you know . . . *legally*.

"That rich legacy doesn't seem to be on Mr. Adams's mind," Gay concludes. "Since the moment the migrants began showing up last

---

* Shannon Thaler, "More Americans Moved Out of This State Than Any Other in 2023: Study," *New York Post*, January 8, 2024, https://nypost.com/2024/01/08 /business/more-americans-moved-out-of-this-state-than-any-other-in-2023/.

spring, he has made clear he wants little to do with the practical or humanitarian issues their arrival has raised. The mayor has provided basic services for the migrants, and rightly so. But at every turn, he has done so grudgingly."

Anyone want to guess how many "asylum seekers" Ms. Gay has taken into her home? It's a number you get when multiplying any other number by zero. How about the sprawling offices of the *New York Times* right across from the bus terminal? Also zero. Point. Zero.

And if you want to see just about the most hypocritical thing perhaps ever, here's Mara Gay in 2020 after Senator Tom Cotton's (R-OK) op-ed in the *New York Times* calling on National Guard troops to be sent into cities where riots get out of control:

"Running this puts black people in danger. And other Americans standing up for our humanity and democracy, too. @nytimes," Gay wrote at the time regarding the op-ed that led to the dismissal of *Times* editor James Bennet after she and other members of the newsroom took to social media to publicly denounce the perfectly reasonable piece.

Fast-forward to March 2024, when New York governor Kathy Hochul (D) ordered 750 National Guard troops into the New York City subway system after violent crime in the tunnels spun completely out of control.

"New York City cannot function without a thriving subway, and ensuring that the system not only is safe but feels safe is paramount. So Gov. Kathy Hochul's decision to deploy 750 National Guard members and 250 New York State Police officers to the subways after a spate of attacks is the right one," Gay argued without a hint of self-awareness.

Overall, the editorial board is about as willingly blind and tone-deaf as any rag out there. The problem is, the Gray Lady is considered the paper of record and the journalistic version of a Bible to Democrats. Check out what they wrote about the border under Trump:

"President Trump is right: There is a crisis at the southern border. Just not the one he rants about. There is no pressing national security threat—no invasion of murderers, drug cartels or terrorists. No matter how often Mr. Trump delivers such warnings, they bear little resemblance to the truth."

No murderers, drug cartels, or terrorists, huh?

Per the *New York Post*, August 2023:

> A trio of armed men were seen crossing the southern border into Texas on Saturday in what is believed to be the latest incident of suspected Mexican cartel members making their way onto US soil.
>
> Startling images of the incident obtained by Fox News show the three suspected cartel gunmen, one of whom appears to be outfitted with body armor, making their way through the South Texas scrubland, near Fronton, with rifles at the ready.
>
> In a similar incident in June, five suspected members of the Cartel Del Noreste were arrested in the same area after illegally crossing the border armed with rifles and tactical gear.

Go figure. But you know, if the *Times* actually deployed a reporter down there once in a blue moon, they might see their assumptions from afar about no threats coming across the border as bad journalism. Maybe if they saw some of the *guns* these guys were carrying, they'd finally be willing to close the border. Last I checked, Democrats still don't like guns. . . .

As for the no-terrorists thing, here's just one of many examples from NBC News in May 2022:

> An Iraqi citizen who entered the U.S. in September 2020 allegedly plotted to kill George W. Bush, even traveling to Dallas to surveil the former president's home, according to an FBI search warrant affidavit obtained by NBC News. The FBI alleges that Shihab Ahmed Shihab, of Columbus, Ohio, wanted to provide material support to the Islamic State terrorist group, telling a confidential FBI source that he wanted to smuggle people into the country "to murder

former President George W. Bush" because he held him responsible for killing numerous Iraqis in the 2003 invasion of the country.

Enough said.

Our worthless national media, with a few exceptions like Fox, have pretended the border crisis doesn't exist, because to do otherwise would mean actually holding Biden accountable. But not until Gov. Ron DeSantis (R-FL) decided to send fifty migrants to Martha's Vineyard did many news organizations start to truly pay attention. Suddenly awakened, the press traveled en masse to the opulent Massachusetts island to cover this atrocity. The headlines were as pathetic as they were predictable.

New York: *"What Happens When a Party Rejects Humanity?"*

Washington Post editorial board: *"DeSantis Stage-Managed His Cruelty for Everyone to See"*

Time: *"If His Martha's Vineyard Stunt Helps DeSantis Politically, What Does That Say about America?"*

CNN: *"While DeSantis Was Flying Legal Asylum Seekers to Martha's Vineyard, Business Owners in His State Were Struggling for Workers"*

Gov. Gavin Newsom (D-CA) actually accused DeSantis of kidnapping, while the migrants themselves, who broke the law (in theory) by crossing the border, are now suing DeSantis and other Florida officials in a class-action lawsuit.

What a country we live in.

The uber-outrage over the safety and well-being of those illegally entering this country is obviously misplaced. And phony. For starters, the Biden administration for many months has been flying planeloads of illegals to places like Westchester, New York, and Jacksonville, Florida, in the dead of night. Why isn't that called kidnapping and human trafficking?

And if we're so concerned about the physical and mental health of those coming here undocumented, why aren't Newsom and AOC and the media blowing up over the more than 750 migrants who died attempting to cross the border in 2022 alone? That's more than two per day, according to the Department of Homeland Security. For context, two hundred people perished trying to cross the border in 2021, or nearly four times less.

"Smuggling organizations are abandoning migrants in remote and dangerous areas, leading to a rise in the number of rescues but also tragically a rise in the number of deaths," Customs and Border Protection said in a statement when the DHS migrant death toll numbers were released. "The terrain along the border is extreme, the summer heat is severe, and the miles of desert migrants must hike after crossing the border in many areas are unforgiving."

And it's not just on the ground, but in the water like the rough Rio Grande. In one week alone in September 2022, nine migrants drowned while attempting to cross the river on the Texas border. *Nine.* And earlier that summer, fifty-three illegal migrants died in the back of a smuggler's truck near San Antonio.

No photo ops for AOC after that tragedy. No comment from Newsom.

Back to the sanctuary island that is the Vineyard: Panic set in once the plane DeSantis sent landed. Massachusetts called in 125 National Guard troops to assist the 50 illegals who had just landed in one of the richest zip codes in the country.

"The island communities are not equipped to provide sustainable accommodation, and state officials developed a plan to deliver a comprehensive humanitarian response," explained Massachusetts governor Charlie Baker.

But. But . . . you said you're a sanctuary state! And just hours later, these poor migrants were lovingly expelled off the island to a military base in Cape Cod instead.

Leave it to CNN to have this takeaway: "'They enriched us.' Migrants' 44-hour Visit Leaves Indelible Mark on Martha's Vineyard."

Yep.

It's easy to become enriched by strangers who were kicked out in less than two days. An indelible mark the Vineyard is still feeling to this day, for sure.

The 2024 election will be crucial on three major fronts. First, if Republicans take the White House, there's a very good chance power in the Senate will flip back to Republicans as well, given that the party simply needs to flip one seat in deep-red Montana, deep-red West Virginia, and increasingly red Ohio. Second, the House, given the map and the weakness of the Democratic brand (not that the Republican brand is all that strong) should also remain in Mike Johnson's capable hands.

If these two things happen, we're talking about a straight flush of power, which is good news for parents who want oversight of their children's education on one front and those who prefer the benefits of American energy independence on a second front. But the third front may be the most crucial: the US southern border can be secured, a border wall may be completed, and the Remain in Mexico policy can be reinstated. Because on this crucial political battlefield, the stakes have never been higher.

Did you know that more than 169 people on the US terror watch list entered this country through said border in 2023 alone? And those are the ones *we know about*. One would think that the more skillful and stealthy terrorists would avoid being apprehended by border officials and simply enter the country undetected.

We all remember the questions asked after 9/11: How did we not see this attack coming? Why didn't we connect the dots that in retrospect should have been connected? Well, guess what: the press and lawmakers are going to stupidly ask those same questions after the next major terror attack occurs and its origins are traced back to the people carrying this out having crossed into the country from the Middle East to Mexico and into here.

We need more guys like Chad Wolf, the former DHS secretary under Trump, in charge: "The numbers continue to get worse with the Biden administration because they simply are not doing one fundamental thing, and that is enforcing the law and bringing deterrence into that system. If individuals are not afraid of getting caught because they are getting released into the country and never removed, guess what? You will continue to see the numbers that we do every day," Wolf warned on Fox News.

"The issue now is that you have hundreds of thousands of folks coming from about 140 different countries because they know what the rest of Americans know is that the border is wide open and there is very little control over it today," he added.

You read that correctly: Illegals are entering here from *140 different countries*. It's a humanitarian and national security crisis the likes of which this country has never seen.

And the worst part: we have an administration that is enabling it all.

John F. Kennedy would be horrified by this dereliction of duty by Joe Biden as commander in chief. In fact, you can even argue that JFK was downright MAGA as our thirty-fifth president. Here's how . . .

CHAPTER 19

JFK: The Original MAGA President

He is one of the most popular presidents in the history of polling. John Fitzgerald Kennedy.

Harvard graduate.

World War II hero.

Journalist.

Pulitzer Prize winner.

Congressman.

Senator.

The thirty-fifth president of the United States.

Yes, he was handsome. Yes, he was the youngest president ever elected, at age forty-three (Teddy Roosevelt was forty-two, but he assumed office after the assassination of William McKinley). And, yes, Jackie O. and his adorable family certainly helped cement that popularity on a personal level. But Kennedy's average approval rating of *70.1 percent* (Gallup) was more the result of his platform, policy, and execution than any of the aforementioned qualities.

And those policies were, well, *MAGA-esque*. They're also the opposite of everything Team Biden and Democrats are attempting to do today. When Kennedy took office in 1961, for example, the country was going through a recession, prompting the new president to make this declaration at the New York Economic Club: "It is a paradoxical truth that tax rates are too high today and tax revenues are too low—and the soundest way to raise revenues in the long run is to cut rates now."

Wait . . . there was a Democratic president who believed the way to raise revenues long-term is for the government to take *less* of taxpayers' hard-earned money to stimulate the economy?

"When consumers purchase more goods, plants use more of their capacity, men are hired instead of laid off, investment increases, and profits are high. Corporate tax rates must also be cut to increase incentives and the availability of investment capital," Kennedy also correctly noted.

When JFK took office, the top marginal tax rate was an insane 91 percent. He presented Congress with a plan to lower that rate to 70 percent and the corporate tax rate from 52 percent to 47 percent.

And it was wildly successful. By 1965, the federal deficit began to shrink. Annual GDP growth went from just 2.6 percent to 6.6 percent. Unemployment dipped from 6.7 percent in 1961 to just 3.8 percent in 1966.

Fast-forward to 2017: Donald Trump echoes Kennedy on the same issue but makes the case in his uniquely rhetorical way. "We're going to cut taxes for the middle class, make the tax code simpler and more fair for everyday Americans, and we are going to bring back the jobs and wealth that have left our country—and most people thought left our country for good," Trump said of his plan to cut the corporate tax rate from 35 to 21 percent.

"There's gridlock in Washington because there's no leadership. So what I'm doing is a large tax cut especially for the middle class and we're going to have a dynamic country," he also said. "We're going to have dynamic economics. And it's going to be something really special. And people are going back to work."

Trump's economy as a result of these tax cuts (along with improved trade deals, reduced regulations, and the move to energy independence) was historic: pre-pandemic, unemployment dropped to 3.5 percent, the lowest since 1969. When Trump left office, inflation was at 1.3 percent.

Those who fell below the poverty line dropped to the lowest level *ever recorded* in 2019. Home buying skyrocketed in response to low interest rates. A gallon of gas cost $2.40 when Trump left office in January 2021. By June 2022, under Biden, a gallon of gas had jumped to nearly $5 on average nationwide, an increase of more than 100 percent.

But wait! How could Trump have succeeded on the economic front after these geniuses in the media declared he would demolish it?

In October 2016, from the *Washington Post* editorial board: "A President Trump could destroy the world economy."

Paul Krugman of the *New York Times* had the best take, however: "Now comes the mother of all adverse effects—and what it brings with it is a regime that will be ignorant of economic policy and hostile to any effort to make it work," Krugman wrote after Trump's victory. "So we are very probably looking at a global recession, with no end in sight. I suppose we could get lucky somehow. But on economics, as on everything else, a terrible thing has just happened."

It's one of life's great mysteries how Krugman somehow once captured the Nobel Prize in economic sciences. Because this is the same guy who also argued that the tax system JFK inherited—the one with the top marginal tax rate of 91 percent—was actually the *right* way to go.

"America in the 1950s made the rich pay their fair share," he argued in 2011. "Yet contrary to right-wing propaganda then and now, it prospered. And we can do that again."

Uh-huh. Right-wing propaganda created a recession, high unemployment, and limited growth at the end of the 1950s. And the booming economy following Kennedy's tax cuts was also something conjured up by the right-wing media machine.

As for the Second Amendment, which almost every Democrat on Capitol Hill would abolish if given the opportunity, here's JFK—who was a lifelong member of the NRA—on this front:

"We need a nation of minutemen," Kennedy declared in 1961, shortly after taking office. "Citizens who are not only prepared to take up arms, but citizens who regard the preservation of freedom as a basic purpose of their daily life, and who are willing to consciously work and sacrifice for that freedom."

A 2023 Gallup poll showed that 49 percent of Democratic voters want to ban the sale of handguns, while just 26 percent of independents and 6 percent of Republican voters feel the same way.

Lieutenant John F. Kennedy served as a PT boat commander in the South Pacific in World War II. He wasn't drafted but volunteered to serve. Kennedy would go on to be a war hero. Per the JFK Presidential Library:

> On August 2, 1943, as PT 109 was running silent to avoid detection it was struck by the Japanese destroyer *Amagiri*. Traveling at 40 knots, the destroyer cut PT 109 in two. The entire crew was thrown into the dark waters. Kennedy towed injured crew member McMahon 4 miles to a small island to the southeast. All eleven survivors made it to the island after having spent a total of fifteen hours in the water. After four days on the island, with the help of a message on a coconut carried by local islanders to an Australian spying on the Japanese they were finally rescued on August 8th.

Just awe-inspiring stuff that earned Kennedy the prestigious Navy and Marine Corps medal for "courage and endurance and excellent leadership that contributed to the saving of several lives and was in keeping with the highest traditions of the United States Naval Service." He also received a Purple Heart for wounds received.

Fast-forward twenty years. Today's commander in chief, Joe Biden, received a total of *five* draft deferments from serving in Vietnam. When finally asked about this in 2008, a spokesperson for Biden said at the time that he was "disqualified from service because of asthma."

But Biden being Biden (see: a pathological liar), here's what he had to say in 2022 about being "appointed" to the Naval Academy in 1965, which of course, *never happened*.

"I was appointed to the academy in 1965 by a senator who I was running against in 1972—never planned it that way. I wasn't old enough to be sworn in. I was only 29 years old when I was running," Biden claimed before explaining why he wanted to be a football star at the University of Delaware (which, to everyone's surprise, never happened) and therefore had to turn down the academy.

"I didn't come to the academy because I wanted to be a football star. And you had a guy named [Roger] Staubach and [Joe] Bellino here. So, I went to Delaware."

Wait! You're telling me we could have been blessed with a backfield including Roger Staubach—Captain America—Joe Bellino, a Heisman Trophy winner, and . . . Joltin' Joe Biden?

Actually, that would have been impossible. For starters, Biden had already graduated from Delaware in 1965. Yes, he was on the Blue Hens' freshman football team, but he quit after the season. He never saw one play on the field with the varsity. Oh, and Biden had a GPA of 1.9 at the time. The future president would later claim to have graduated at the top of his law class at Syracuse. He actually finished seventy-sixth out of eighty-five students.

So, you want to know how much Democrats have changed from being about helping those who need it most to being about, well, themselves and the celebrity perks that go along with the privileges of power? I give you the postpresidential lives of Jimmy Carter and Barack Obama.

According to Habitat for Humanity, more than 4,300 homes are called "Carter houses" because the former president has helped build that many homes over nearly forty years in fourteen countries. This isn't a write-a-big-check-and-take-a-photo approach to charity; this is showing up and doing the hard work over decades to make the world a better place for those in need. Carter, of course, was a one-term president. He lost in a landslide in 1980. He could have been bitter or embarrassed and left the stage quietly. Instead, he continued to lead by example.

In August 1980, Carter stood at just 32 percent approval just three months before his defeat, the lowest approval rating in Gallup's history. But in doing so much charity work since exiting the Oval, Carter completely changed his standing with the public. By 1999 his approval stood at 66 percent. In 2002 he won the Nobel Peace Prize.[*]

"Jimmy Carter is being seen as one of the great humanitarian and state persons of the 20th and 21st century," historian David Brinkley once proclaimed. He's not wrong.

Barack Obama enjoyed a much different presidency than Carter, mostly thanks to a slobbering love affair with the media, to quote a book by the great Bernie Goldberg. The former community organizer could do no wrong. His speeches were described as electric. He, as the first Black president, was historic.

Numbers? Results? Who cares?

The Obama presidency, if looked at objectively, was the very definition of below average. Economic growth was anemic, with GDP growth over his eight years in office clocking in at just 1.62 percent on average. The nation's debt nearly doubled. ISIS went from what Obama described as a "JV team" to a massive caliphate, killing more than thirty-three thousand people in terror attacks in just a few short years.

And the Democratic brand suffered thanks to Obama's nonexistent coattails. When he took office in 2009, Democrats held 256 seats in the House. Upon his leaving office, that number had dropped to 194. In 2009, Democrats held fifty-eight Senate seats, only to drop to forty-eight by 2017. Democrats even held a majority of governorships (twenty-eight out of fifty states), but that number dropped to eighteen by the end of Obama's second term.

When the Obamas left the White House, some predicted the postpresidency of the First Couple would mirror that of the Carters.

---

[*] "Jimmy Carter Improves with Age," news release, ABC News, October 1, 1999, https://abcnews.go.com/images/pdf/796a10Carter.pdf.

Obama was a community organizer, after all, so the argument was that he would return to his roots, perhaps in his home city of Chicago.

Instead, the Obamas signed with Netflix as producers. They vacationed with CBS News "journalist" Gayle King, which isn't a conflict of interest or anything on her part. Michelle even launched a podcast (because who doesn't have one these days?). And here's a description of their Martha's Vineyard mansion, per *Homes & Gardens*:

> The Taylor Lombardo–designed estate spans 6,892 square feet on this celebrity-approved island—and features seven bedrooms, eight and a half baths, and a host of architectural qualities—such as wood-paneled ceilings and several stone fireplaces. The property also includes access to a pond and includes a boat house and a private beachfront with deeded rights. It sits on nearly 30 verdant acres fronting the Edgartown Great Pond between Slough Cove and Turkeyland Cove and comes with views of the Atlantic as standard.

So while Carter built homes, the Obamas purchased one the size of Soldier Field. The former president is also getting his own library being built on Chicago's South Side. Other presidents, like FDR and Reagan, also have libraries, so this isn't a new development. What *is* new is the cost: according to the Obama Presidential Center's annual report, when all is said and done, the library will take north of $825 million to construct.*

Crime in Chicago, meanwhile, is completely and totally out of control. In 2022 it had more murders than Los Angeles and New Orleans *combined*.

Many of these murders were carried out by young adults and teen-

---

* Marina Fang, "Obama's Presidential Library Could Cost $1 Billion: Report," HuffPost, August 16, 2015, https://www.huffpost.com/entry/obama-presidential-library_n_55d 1134be4b055a6dab0a54f.

agers, many of whom had left the Chicago school system. According to the independent nonprofit research firm Wirepoints, state data reveals that not one of the eighty-eight students at Spry Community Links High School in Chicago can read at grade level or is proficient in math.

Not. One.

As in: Zero.

Per Wirepoints: "Spry is one of 30 schools in Illinois where not a single student can read at grade level. Twenty-two of those schools are part of the Chicago Public Schools and the other eight are outside Chicago."

So, perhaps, I don't know . . . instead of raising a cool billion to build a shrine to yourself, Mr. Obama, how about donating $800 million of it to these thirty schools to allow them to hire top teachers and tutors and improve school security and resources? There would still be millions left over, which should suffice to erect a library celebrating your largely listless presidency. And when you're done signing that check, perhaps the former First Lady and you can volunteer to teach at these schools while actively fundraising, which you were exceptionally accomplished at during said presidency.

This will never happen, of course. Because this is the press the Obamas are generating these days. And it has zero to do with murders or illiteracy.

Deadline: *"Ex-President Obama earned a nomination this morning as Outstanding Narrator for his work on the Netflix documentary series* Working: What We Do All Day. *The 44th president is the defending champion in that category, after winning in 2022 for narrating the Netflix series* Our Great National Parks.*"*

People: *"Michelle Obama is now an Emmy-nominated producer. The former first lady, 59, received her first-ever Emmy nomination on Wednesday for outstanding nonfiction series or special for Netflix's* The Light We Carry: Michelle Obama & Oprah Winfrey.*"*

Carter. Obama. Two subpar presidents. And if someone more like Reagan and less like Romney ran against the latter in 2012, both would have the distinction of being one-term presidents. But at least one of them showed he truly cared about the plights of the less fortunate, while the other polishes his Emmy Award.

Neither, of course, compared to John Fitzgerald Kennedy. If you need any more proof of how much Democratic presidents have changed, check out these very telling quotes about taking responsibility for one's actions when things go horribly wrong.

White House statement, April 24, 1961, following the failed US-backed Bay of Pigs military mission in Cuba to overthrow Fidel Castro and the Communist government:

"President Kennedy has stated from the beginning that as president he bears sole responsibility for the events of the past few days. He has stated it on all occasions & he restates it now so that it will be understood by all."

He bears sole responsibility. No excuses. No deflection. No lies.

President Joe Biden, August 31, 2021, following the chaotic and deadly withdrawal of US forces that included thirteen US service members killed by an ISIS-K suicide bomber in front of Kabul International Airport:

"The extraordinary success of this mission was due to the incredible skill, bravery, and selfless courage of the United States military and our diplomats and intelligence professionals."

Extraordinary success. . . .

"The previous administration's agreement said that if we stuck to the May 1st deadline that they had signed on to leave by, the Taliban wouldn't attack any American forces, but if we stayed, all bets were off," Biden also said. "So we were left with a simple decision: Either follow through on the commitment made by the last administration and leave Afghanistan, or say we weren't leaving and commit another tens of thousands more troops going back to war."

You see? Biden had *no choice* but to stick to Trump's agreement with the Taliban and the timelines that were set. *He's* the victim here. *Trump* is to blame. Of course, Biden signed dozens of executive orders reversing almost every Trump initiative and policy within weeks after taking office, but that Taliban agreement he could have easily renegotiated? That was like herpes, apparently. He and his team were stuck with it.

So, to sum it up, Kennedy took sole responsibility for the Bay of Pigs operation (which was drawn up by the Eisenhower administration), while Biden somehow took a victory lap after thirteen US service members came home in coffins while simultaneously blaming his predecessor for their deaths.

Just absolutely appalling, and that's being generous.

JFK, the most popular president in modern political history, was just getting started with the original America First agenda (low taxes to grow the economy, an expanded and stronger military, opposition to racial quotas, which we'll dive into later in the book) when that fateful day in Dallas in November 1963 stopped what could have been the greatest eight years any president ever had.

Back to the future, Kennedy's nephew, Robert F. Kennedy Jr., launched his campaign for president in the spring of 2023. But the modern-day press and Democratic Party aren't exactly embracing Camelot this time around. Not even close. Instead, it is embracing authoritarianism while claiming to be protectors of democracy. It's enough to make your hair hurt. . . .

PART V

Remember When Democrats Cared about the Whole Truth?

We hear lots of talk about the dangers of disinformation from the very media who are the biggest purveyors of it. It wasn't always this way, of course. There was even a time when the most trusted man in America was the anchor of *CBS Evening News*. And, no, we're not talking about Dan Rather.

But even the once-venerable *60 Minutes* has lost its credibility in the age of Trump. CNN, also once a respected news organization, saw its own woke employees stage an insurrection against its own president for having the audacity to host a town hall for Trump. MSNBC? Please. It's like taking *The View* and making it a twenty-four-hour program while somehow being more unhinged, if that's humanly possible. Even much of our sports media, once my dojo, has gone off the deep end to the left.

In the end, it's good to be a Democrat, with so many friends to promote and protect you on traditional and social media and even in the sports pages. We break down the good, the bad, and especially the ugly in our next section.

CHAPTER 20

Dem Damn Authoritarians "Defending" Democracy

Hand in hand with freedom of speech goes the power to be heard, to share in the decisions of government which shape men's lives.
—ROBERT F. KENNEDY SR.

If you're in the mood to be disturbed or horrified, you've come to the right chapter! Because according to an August 2023 poll conducted by Pew Research, *a majority* of Americans believe the US government should be in the business of censoring information online it deems to be false. The new majority is driven by Democrats, as 70 percent of those voters support the federal government censoring online content.

"Support for government intervention has steadily risen since the first time we asked this question in 2018. In fact, the balance of opinion has tilted: Five years ago, Americans were more inclined to prioritize freedom of information over restricting false information (58% vs. 39%)," Pew reported.

"Democrats and Democratic-leaning independents are much more likely than Republicans and Republican leaners to support the U.S. government taking steps to restrict false information online (70% vs. 39%). There was virtually no difference between the parties in 2018, but the share of Democrats who support government intervention has grown from 40% in 2018 to 70% in 2023," it added.

You read that correctly: it was just five years ago that four in ten Democrats believed in government censorship of information online. It's just stunning to see a number regarding the very bedrock of our republic, free speech, take a hit like this.

Perhaps these Democrats are watching too much *Morning Joe* on MSNBC, because this 2017 quote from cohost Mika Brzezinski stands out in a sea of insanity on that network:

"I think that the dangerous edges here are that [Trump] is trying to undermine the media, trying to make up his own facts. And it could be that while unemployment and the economy worsens, he could have undermined the messaging so much that he can actually control exactly what people think. And that . . . that is our job," she said.

Controlling exactly what people think is the media's job? Well, butter my butt and call me a biscuit. But it's a true sentiment that so many in this industry have: *they* are the final authority on truth.

Or perhaps Democrat voters are listening to former CNN senior media correspondent Brian Stelter.

Much like Mika, and the rest of the liberal establishment, Stelter really believes his own BS. And to that end, the World Economic Forum chose Stelter in 2023—months after his show was canceled by CNN—to moderate a panel with a name that sounded like a John Clancy novel: "The Clear & Present Danger of Disinformation."

During the panel, the vice president for values and transparency at the European Commission, Věra Jourová, declared that hate speech will become criminalized in the United States in the near future:

"Illegal hate speech, which you will have soon also in the U.S., I think that we have a strong reason why we have this in the criminal law."

Stelter just nodded along like it was bobblehead night. Yup. Criminalizing hate speech is *good*. But how does one define "hate speech," and who gets to play judge and jury on sending people to jail over it?

Toward the end of the Trump presidency, NPR's Terry Gross asked

Stelter (who was CNN's media reporter at the time) why he, as a person who insists he's an objective journalist, is injecting his opinions more into his reporting.

"In 10 or 20 years, I want to be able to look back and be proud of how I covered the Trump presidency," Stelter told Gross. "I think that's the ultimate test for any journalist right now. Will you be proud of what you said and what you did? I have definitely been outspoken on *Reliable Sources*. I've been doing more monologues than I used to, and so have a lot of other CNN anchors."

He added: "Sometimes talking straight to the camera and explaining what the president did or didn't do, explaining how we know it's a lie, I think that's more effective than having a debate between two talking heads or falling for that both-sides trap because, Terry, there are certain things that we have to stand up for. Truth and decency and democracy, those are not partisan values. They should never be viewed as partisan values."

If you just threw up in your mouth a little, you're not alone. Because never *once* did Stelter ever apply the word *lie* to Joe Biden, who has a very long history of telling blatant, easily fact-checked lies to the American people. One could even write an entire bestselling book on it (shameless, I know).

So let's put this to an easy test: let's say Stelter invited a psychiatrist on his show to talk about Trump's mental fitness. The shrink, Dr. Allen Francis, had on numerous occasions sounded like Rob Reiner on his Twitter feed in ranting about how horrible Trump was. Stelter invited him on for that reason: to push a narrative in what was a fixed segment.

"Trump is as destructive a person in this century as Hitler, Stalin, Mao were in the last century," Francis told Stelter in 2019 in a segment that actually happened on the now-defunct *Reliable Sources*. "He may be responsible for many more million deaths than they were."

Wow. Did you hear that? A psychiatrist from Duke University said, without ambiguity, on *national television*, that the sitting president of the United States had killed more people than *Hitler, Stalin, and Mao.*

That's talking in the range of more than 100 million people, or almost one-third of the entire US population!

If this isn't the easiest fact-check in the history of fact-checks for any "journalist" whose mission statement is to expose falsehood, I'm not sure what is.

So what did Stelter do or say after that statement? Absolutely nothing. And when called out on it on social media, he lied when making an excuse for not pushing back.

"I agree that I should have interrupted after that line. I wish I had heard him say it, but I was distracted by tech difficulties," Stelter responded on Twitter.

Reliable Sources? You've got to be kidding me.

The *Babylon Bee* couldn't come up with something more absurd. Anyone who works in television knows this is a lie, and a bad one at that. In reviewing the entire program, the questions and answers between host and guests were seamless. Dr. Francis didn't join by Skype or Zoom (this was pre-pandemic, when that was far less common), but from a professional studio in Philadelphia. Stelter's expression of listening intently doesn't change once throughout the interview. He heard everything, and to believe only that moment when Francis blamed Trump for killing *tens and tens of millions of people* is the exact moment the audio went out is laughable. And if there was a technical issue, Stelter wouldn't have waited until the blowback was too much to ignore before addressing it on Twitter; he would have done so after the next commercial break, upon being informed what the guest actually said.

Of course, this is also the same "reporter" who claimed that "entire media companies essentially exist to tear down Joe Biden" before asking a guest on his show if "there is an equivalent of that on the Left, tearing down Trump?"

Gee, I don't know. Could the answer be . . . CNN?

As for truth, here's all you need to know, from his own words.

Stelter in October 2020, on the *New York Post*'s reporting on Hunter

Biden's laptop (emphasis mine): "This is a classic example of *the right-wing media machine*. Fox and Trump have this in common: They want you to stay mad and stay tuned."

"Now, let's pull up Don Junior's tweet from just a little while ago," Stelter later added in reference to Donald Trump Jr.'s tweet challenging the media to cover this bombshell from the *New York Post*. "'How—'" he says, "'How will the media attempt to sweep this one under the rug?'

"That is the *meta-narrative*. That's the big story they're telling," the media correspondent declared. "It's all about *grievance and bias and victimhood*. So, let's talk about the significance of *these manufactured scandals* with [Harvard Professor] Yochai Benkler."

But here's Stelter in a February 2023 interview with *Fourth Watch* podcast host Steve Krakauer, an actual journalist who once worked for CNN. Krakauer pressed Stelter on his dismissal of the damning contents of Biden's laptop and calling the story a "right-wing media" creation, but Stelter tried to spin reality differently three years later:

"A lot of the lies that happen now about what happened in 2020," he said, "go like this—they say, 'All these assholes, they all called it disinformation!' That's not true!"

Stelter had literally called it a "manufactured scandal." It's on tape and everything.

He wasn't done.

"A lot of us just wondered, we said out loud, 'could this be?' We said things like 'some former U.S. officials think it might be,' it was always cushioned—it was not always, it was often cushioned that way," Stelter went on, before adding this doozy: "And now in retrospect, two years later, three years later, people like partisans like to pretend that it was labeled disinformation, which it wasn't."

No, it was labeled disinformation by Brian himself. Yep. This is the guy who gets hired to moderate panels on "The Clear & Present Danger of Disinformation."

Oh, that'll never really happen here in the United States, you say? Because it is, and then some, under Team Biden.

Just ask federal judge Terry Doughty, who slammed the administration for carrying out "the most massive attack against free speech in United States' history."

Doughty said in a scathing ruling that the Biden administration actively pressured social media giants "to censor misinformation regarding climate change, gender discussions, abortion, economic policy," along with COVID-19.

Within days after Biden was inaugurated, White House digital director Rob Flaherty scolded Twitter and demanded it "immediately" take down a parody account of Biden's relatives. Twitter obeyed in forty-five minutes. Again, this was a *parody account*.

In a related story, who was the leader who spread *this* kind of misinformation on national television?

"There's a simple, basic proposition: If you're vaccinated, you're not going to be hospitalized, you're not going to be in an ICU unit, and you're not going to die.

"You're not going to—you're not going to get COVID if you have these vaccinations."

Answer: President Joseph Robinette Biden on (ding! ding! ding!) CNN in 2021. There was no *Reliable Sources* segment calling out the president's lies the following Sunday. And as we know, vaccines don't prevent an individual from getting Covid. They don't keep everyone who gets infected out of the hospital. And some vaccinated people have died from Covid. Not an opinion. That's based on data.

But the Biden administration says the government should play judge and jury on what is truth and what is falsehood. You know, perhaps censorship in the name of fighting "misinformation" is being embraced by the left because they're being taught in young adulthood that there is "good speech" (if a liberal says it) and "bad speech" (if a conservative says it).

On that note, did you know that when it comes to commencement speeches at the top-hundred-ranked universities in the country, only *three* had someone considered to be a conservative speaker in 2022?

Of those three conservatives, one of them was Tim Tebow at the University of Florida. Pretty sure a national championship and a Heisman Trophy earned him that gig in Gainesville. Another was Glenn Youngkin, the governor of Virginia, at a school in the especially red part of the state—Virginia Tech in Blacksburg. The third conservative was the prime minister of Greece (whoever that is) at Boston College. And that's it.

It wasn't always this way. President Reagan delivered nine commencement speeches during his presidency on campuses ranging from Tuskegee University to Notre Dame with little to no uproar. But now if Ben Shapiro or Candace Owens or Charlie Kirk attempts to speak on campus, they're met not just with protest but sometimes even with violence.

A Brookings Institution survey shows that 62 percent of college students who identify as Democrats believe it is acceptable to shout down a speaker they disagree with on campus. From there, it gets worse, with 19 percent (basically one in five) of students overall saying that violence is justified to shut down a speaker.

Meanwhile, here's the definition of what it means to be a progressive, per the *Cambridge Dictionary*: "People who are willing to consider new ideas or different ideas from their own before making a decision or a judgment."

Yep. Nothing says being willing to consider new or different ideas from their own before passing judgment quite like shouting down or physically assaulting someone you disagree with.

OK, so let's say there are still some journalists who graduate and want to do solid investigative work and hold the powerful accountable without fear or favor to party. Many of them will be working in either New York or Washington—two of the bluest cities in the country. And most will adapt to their liberal environments quickly, in the name of career survival. Because if they actually start holding Democrats accountable, for example, they could get threatened or eliminated.

Look at what happened to Matt Taibbi, who handled the Twitter files, along with Bari Weiss and Michael Shellenberger.

Taibbi testified on Capitol Hill in 2023. But Stacey Plaskett, a Democrat—and the ranking member of the House Judiciary Select Subcommittee on the Weaponization of the Federal Government—threatened Taibbi with jail time for a minor mistake. As in *five years of jail time*.

During his testimony, Taibbi explained how Twitter executives took orders from CISA (the Cybersecurity and Infrastructure Security Agency) about tweets that should be censored but had his government agency acronyms slightly confused during his testimony, as he meant to reference CIS (the Center for Internet Security). "Effectively, news media became an arm of a state-sponsored thought-policing system," Taibbi wrote in his report in naming multiple agencies and entities he concluded were involved in this thought-policing system, including the FBI, DHS, HHS, DOD, and CIA, among others, including CISA.

Taibbi's reference to CISA was a simple matter of applying the wrong acronym (off by one letter) to a government agency, as he meant to refer to CIS.

Taibbi later corrected the error in his reporting. But for Plaskett, that wasn't good enough. "Under the federal perjury statute . . . providing false information is punishable by up to five years imprisonment," she warned.

Five years for getting an acronym wrong? Can you imagine if Jim Acosta was threatened with jail time by anyone in the previous administration? The fainting-couch store would run out of fainting couches.

You know, if a socialist idea is being bandied about in Washington, there must be some kind of connection back to its most famous Democratic socialist: AOC. Here she is in 2018 on the need for government-run "media literacy" for all Americans:

"There's absolutely a commission that's being discussed, but it seems to be more investigating in style rather than truth and reconciliation," Ocasio-Cortez said in an Instagram video at the time. "I do think that several members of Congress in some of my discussions have brought up media literacy because that is part of what happened here. We're going to have to figure out how we rein in our media environment so you can't just spew disinformation and misinformation."

Rein in our media environment. Comforting coming from AOC. Here's what she said in a 2018 *60 Minutes* interview when asked about how she's been fact-checked around dubious claims in public comments:

"If people want to really blow up one figure here or one word there, I would argue that they're missing the forest for the trees. I think that there's a lot of people more concerned about being precisely, factually and semantically correct than about being morally right," she told Anderson Cooper. "That's an utterly fascinating way to define truth: Hey. It's not that big of a deal to be factually correct, so as long as a person is, from their own perspective, *morally right.*"

It's just so hilarious to think about how many times Democrats have pushed the panic button in order to instill fear in the American voter. Remember the alarm bells over the Trump-era repeal of net neutrality?

"End of the Internet as We Know It," CNN.com declared briefly after the FCC voted 3–2 along party lines in 2017 to do away with its Open Internet Order, implemented during the Obama administration.

"Trump's FCC Repeals Obama-Era Net Neutrality Regulations Intended to Keep the Web Open and Fair," read the CNN sub-headline on its home page. And this wasn't even an opinion piece.

Democrats joined together to declare Internet Armageddon in an open letter released right before the 3–2 vote. "By overturning the commission's current rules that preserve net neutrality and prevent internet service providers from blocking, throttling, or otherwise privileging lawful content, we fear that the Draft Order could harm our nation's students and schools—especially those in rural and low-income communities," the letter reads.

And then a funny thing happened. Or in this case, didn't happen. None of what Democrats and their allies at CNN said would happen came true.

"It is not going to destroy the internet. It is not going to end the internet as we know it. It is not going to kill democracy. It is not going to stifle free expression online," said FCC commissioner Ajit Pai after the vote. And it didn't. But then, once social media giants like Facebook and Twitter began picking and choosing what speech could be blocked, suppressed, and censored, Democrats and many in the media cheered. All in the name of protecting democracy, of course.

The Biden administration says it wants to battle misinformation. The best place to start may be purchasing a large mirror. Because when you blame Putin's invasion of Ukraine for inflation that has been rising for well over a year, or blame Trump for the current state of the US border, or say democracy is at stake if voting rights aren't federalized, maybe the arbiters-of-truth business isn't one you should be in.

"You are entitled to your opinion. But you are not entitled to your own facts." That's a great quote from the late Democrat senator Daniel Patrick Moynihan of New York.

Speaking of which, our sports media used to be a show largely free of partisan opinion that focused on following the facts. But this ain't your daddy's sports media anymore. Here's how and why . . .

CHAPTER 21

Our Insufferably Woke Sports Media

There was a time when America's pastime showed a weariness of Florida's hostile approach to inclusiveness, which in some ways is being reconstituted by its current governor, Ron DeSantis."
Multiple choice time again! Did the paragraph above come from . . .

a) Politico
b) *The* New York Times
c) *Axios*
d) CNN
e) *None of the above*

If you went with e, my college go-to, you're correct! It actually comes from ESPN's Kevin Blackistone, who also serves as a sports columnist for the *Washington Post.*

And Blackistone wasn't through with his rant against the Florida governor while putting on his activist hat: "If baseball is still concerned with as much, its 15 franchises that started spring training last month in Florida should consider making the annual exercise an all–Cactus League affair as long as [Gov. Ron] DeSantis commands an attack on diversity."

You read that right: a sports columnist is demanding a professional sports league uproot *fifteen franchises* because he disagrees with a Republican governor's stance on education. And by all means, dismiss what such moves would do to Florida spring training towns and cities from an economic and jobs perspective (see: Devastating). Why? Because Blackistone *really* wants to teach DeSantis a lesson regarding his state's decision to modify certain elements of an advanced placement high school course on African American studies.

For his part, DeSantis, along with the state's nonprofit College Board, has called parts of the course "indoctrination," because part of this course on African American history included something called "Queer Theory."

"This is a course on Black history—what's one of the lessons about? Queer theory," DeSantis explained to reporters in March 2023. "Now, who would say that an important part of Black history is queer theory? That is somebody pushing an agenda on our kids."

He's correct. What exactly does sexual orientation have to do with Black history?

Another part of the course that DeSantis and the College Board took issue with was the inclusion of Black Lives Matter. Is that political organization really a part of Black history? Because as you may have heard, BLM has seen a serious drop in public approval thanks to internal scandals around how some of its leaders have spent millions in donations on mansions while also facing a lawsuit from another BLM organization (BLM Grassroots) alleging that one of its executives from the BLM Global Network Foundation has "syphoned" more than $10 million from donors. Yup, let's hoist this crooked organization on a pedestal.

By the way, the AP course, post-modification, still includes actual Black history, including the transatlantic slave trade, the Thirteenth Amendment, and Frederick Douglass. Students should learn about American history, the good, the bad, and the ugly, in order to learn from our (sometimes horrific) past mistakes and avoid repeating them.

"We proudly require the teaching of African American history,"

Florida commissioner of education Manny Diaz Jr. posted on Twitter at the time. "We do not accept woke indoctrination masquerading as education."

If this sounds familiar, it's because it is reminiscent of some in sports media beclowning themselves in demanding that the MLB All-Star Game be moved out of Atlanta because of new voting laws passed in 2021. According to them, minority voters were going to be suppressed. Voting would be made harder to the point it would impact turnout and morale. And despite not doing the most basic homework around the bill, MLB commissioner Rob Manfred decided to move the game to lily-white Denver instead.

"By making this move, Manfred has put other leagues on notice as long as Georgia insists on standing by this bill," *USA Today* sports columnist Bob Nightengale wrote after the announcement to move the game was made, and then took it three ridiculous steps further.

"The NFL surely can't give Atlanta another Super Bowl," he declared. "Same goes for the NBA and its All-Star Game. And the NCAA and the Final Four."

Why not demand that the University of Georgia just move out of Georgia while you're at it, Bob?

The move by MLB cost local businesses in Atlanta, many minority-owned, up to $100 million in revenue, according to the Job Creators Network. Oh, and despite the claim that voters would be suppressed under the new law, Georgia has easily *broken voting records* in two major elections held since.

MLB never apologized to those Georgia businesses. And Nightengale continues to be insufferable on a regular basis in writing for *USA Today*. But in the best irony ever, the Atlanta Braves won the World Series in the same year the All-Star Game was moved out of their stadium, which helped recoup some of the revenue lost after the July game was moved to Colorado.

In the end, most sports fans simply want to go to a game to be entertained, to watch the best players in the world engage in a sport that has been a part of this country's fabric for nearly 150 years. But Major League Baseball, along with Coca-Cola and Delta Airlines, decided to pick a side here, while pushing a demonstrably false narrative by President Biden and his allies in the media that the new Georgia law was "Jim Crow 2.0."

And instead of covering the Braves' incredible run to their first championship since 1995, Nightengale again played the outrage card over Atlanta's nickname. "While I can't stop the tomahawk chop or make Atlanta change its name, what I can do is not acknowledge the nickname," Nightengale wrote before the Braves clinched the series over Houston in Game 6. "In recent years, I have tried to avoid using Atlanta's nickname in columns. I find it offensive."

Just spitballing here, but do you get the feeling that we'll soon see a screed from guys like this over the New York Jets needing to change their name? Because jet engines cause pollution and leave a huge carbon footprint, and that simply cannot happen. They should be called the New York Scooters instead.

Up the road from the Peach State, we all saw what happened in Washington, a city that once had an NFL team called the Redskins, established in 1932. And for decades upon decades, *not one peep* was said about the team nickname, especially from Native Americans.

But then one day, about ten years ago, some sportswriters declared the name *was* offensive. It must be changed. These same writers were about as Native American as Elizabeth Warren, of course, but no matter.

So as the uproar that was confined to sports columnists began to grow, thanks to conformity and virtue signaling, the *Washington Post* decided to do a poll on the matter in 2016. Here's what they found: *nine out of ten* Native Americans had no problem with the Washington Redskins as a team name.

Another poll three years later during the Trump presidency, also from the *Post*, found that Native Americans picked the word *proud* first regarding the Redskins' team name. Overall, across the country, just 29 percent favored changing the Redskins' name.

Back in 2013, President Obama, who hadn't said one word about the Redskins' name during the first four years of his presidency or at any time during his previous stints as a US senator or community organizer, weighed in on the contrived controversy.

"If I were the owner of the team and I knew that there was a name of my team—even if it had a storied history—that was offending a sizeable group of people, I'd think about changing it," Obama said in an interview published by the Associated Press.

But that's the problem. A sizable group of people were apathetic about the name. The same Associated Press did a survey not long after Obama's comments that year, and just 11 percent said the name should be changed.

Never to let a contrived crisis go to waste, more Democrats jumped on board; in 2014 forty-nine Democratic senators penned a stern letter to NFL commissioner Roger Goodell to change the name.

"We urge you and the National Football League to send the same clear message as the NBA did: that racism and bigotry have no place in professional sports," read the letter, whose signees included Sen. Elizabeth Warren (D–Cherokee Nation).

Redskins owner Daniel Snyder was steadfast in keeping the Redskins' name, as was former Chicago Bears coach Mike Ditka, a guy who was once paid to give his unfiltered opinions on NBC.

"What's all the stink over the Redskin name? It's so much shit it's incredible," Ditka said in an interview with Mike Richman of Redskins Historian.com in 2014.

We're going to let the liberals of the world run this world. It was said out of reverence, out of pride to the American Indian. Even though it was called a Redskin, what are you going to call them, a Proudskin? This is so stupid it's appalling, and I hope that owner keeps fighting for it and never changes it, because the Redskins are part of an American football history, and it should never be anything but the Washington Redskins. That's the way it is.

It's been the name of the team since the beginning of football. It has nothing to do with something that happened lately, or something that somebody dreamed up. This was the name, period. Leave it alone. These people are silly—asinine, actually, in my opinion.

Not long after those comments, Ditka called Obama "the worst president we've ever had." For ESPN, that was *way* over the line, and they promptly removed Ditka from ESPN's NFL pregame show.

The network, however, did not do the same when *Pardon the Interruption* host Tony Kornheiser likened Republican lawmakers to ISIS, nor did they issue any reprimand of then *SportsCenter* anchor Kenny Mayne, who once declared he wanted to ram a car that had a Sarah Palin sticker on it, but decided against doing so because "there may be kids in the car."

Another example of sports media being profoundly political involves transgender swimmer Lia Thomas, the broad-shouldered biological male who dominated women's swimming at the University of Pennsylvania in the early 2020s. Thomas, as a male, was ranked *462nd in the country* at Penn. But after he decided to transition to a she, Thomas jumped all the way up to number one on the women's side in winning a national championship.

"She should be embraced in the history of progress that sports represent and recognized as the trailblazer that she is," NBC's Cheryl Cooky swooned after Thomas's victory (Cooky would actually go on to compare Thomas to Jackie Robinson, who broke baseball's color barrier in 1947).

What is hard to find in coverage surrounding Thomas's rise is the biological advantages she possesses over other female swimmers. Here's an exception per *Swimming World* magazine's John Lohn:

"What we are stating is this: The effects of being born a biological male, as they relate to the sport of swimming, offer Thomas a clear-cut edge over the biological females against whom she is competing. She is stronger. It is that simple. And this strength is beneficial to her stroke, on turns and to her endurance. Doping has the same effect."

And that's so spot-on. The advantages Thomas has are no different than those of athletes who take steroids or human growth hormones (HGH). But because so many Democratic sports columnists are afraid of being attacked by the woke mob, and perhaps even by their pious peers, as somehow being transphobic for pointing this out, almost all have avoided weighing in on it.

Thomas, of course, is still a man. This person hasn't had gender re-assignment surgery as of 2023 and is allowed to race against young women half his/her size. And before one race, Thomas decided to show off his/her body parts to other swimmers on the women's team.

"In that locker room, we turned around and there's a 6'1" biological man dropping his pants and watching us undress, and we were exposed to male genitalia," shared University of Kentucky swimmer Riley Gaines. "We did not give our consent, they did not ask for our consent."

Gaines would go on to do a speech on campus at San Francisco State University. Check that: she *attempted* to speak. But a mob of protesters not only shouted her down but actually physically engaged her, eventually cornering her in a classroom where she had to barricade herself until security could get her out safely.

Most of the media stayed silent, offering no coverage.

"I was physically assaulted by one person. I was struck twice, both times hitting my shoulder with the second strike grazing my face," Gaines shared afterward. "The rest of the protestors just ambushed and cornered me before I was able to move out with the help of campus police."

But don't tell that to the University of Pennsylvania, who nominated Thomas for its NCAA Woman of the Year award.

Personal note: My wife, Jean, ran track at Georgetown. Division 1. Full scholarship. It was needed, too, as her father suffered a massive heart attack when she was young and he was only in his thirties. Bill

Readie, who legally immigrated to the United States as a young boy from Scotland during World War II to escape the bombings, was the quintessential blue-collar guy. He worked tough jobs at printing presses at companies in the swamps near the old Giants Stadium in North Jersey. But after the heart attack and triple bypass surgery, he couldn't do anything requiring the sweat and effort that goes into running printing presses. He would go on to work odd jobs for the rest of his life but never quit earning for his family by any means necessary.

Money was obviously tight in their small two-bedroom, one-bathroom home in Lyndhurst, New Jersey. And by the time their youngest daughter of three, the aforementioned Jean, was ready to go to college, affording Georgetown, one of the most expensive universities in the country, was basically off the table.

But my wife is a gazelle, having been highly ranked in the country in the 600 meters in high school at one point. And Georgetown had one of the top track teams in D-1, along with an outstanding premed program. Jean knew she wanted to be a doctor after witnessing her father have that heart attack right in front of her when she was a little girl, and didn't want to have that feeling of helplessness again.

Fast-forward to 2023, and my wife still serves as an emergency physician. Running is no longer the best option, two torn MCLs later, but she still gets her miles in on the exercise bike, which is easier on the knees. She's also the proud mother of our two kids, Cameron, ten, and Liam, eight. So between working and shuttling two very active kids from everything to soccer to basketball to football to track, the day is always busy and doesn't leave much time for reading about or watching the political scene.

But when it comes to the Lia Thomas story, that's about the only time I see Jean passionate about political debate. She knows exactly how hard it is to make it onto any college team at that level, and the sacrifices she had to make in terms of training, which is grueling, all while enduring medical classes, which are equally grueling.

Could you imagine, she asks, being a girl who worked almost her entire life to earn a scholarship to a Division 1 school? And after grueling practice after grueling practice for hours almost every day year-round, and gutting out win after win, you make it to the conference or NCAA Finals for your category. But going into the championship race, you already know the competition is fixed. You *know* you're going to lose. Because as you look across the blocks right before diving into the water, you see a *six-foot-one guy* posing as a girl who looks like he/she could play running back for the college football team racing against you. You already read what racing times Thomas posted that year, and you *know* you haven't raced that fast in your entire career. This thing is over even before it begins.

"How do you think she feels?" Jean asks.

Remember the East German swimmers back in the Olympics who looked like the offensive line for the Washington Redskins, er, Commanders? They were condemned by the international community for doping. They were called cheaters because they were. Same goes for Mark McGwire and Sammy Sosa and Barry Bonds and Alex Rodriguez and Roger Clemens and hundreds of other professionals who many fans and sportswriters felt had cheated by taking steroids and HGH during their baseball careers (Sosa and Clemens still deny the allegations). Either way, sports columnists had zero issues about calling them out.

But with Lia Thomas, this is like the third rail of topics for these folks. Why? Because the woke mob on Twitter will come for anyone who dares raise these valid points around cheating.

What effing cowards.

Fortunately, there are financial ramifications for this effort to inject activism into sports journalism. ESPN, for example, which took a big turn to the left in recent years, has seen a major loss of viewers who feel the organization has become too vocal in supporting liberal causes while taking the escapism out of watching sports.

At any given time, tune to the self-described "Worldwide Leader in Sports" and be subjected to anchors, I don't know . . . fighting back tears talking about the Supreme Court decision to overturn *Roe v. Wade*.

"Today, the Supreme Court overturned *Roe vs. Wade*, declaring that the constitutional right to abortion, upheld for nearly a half-century, no longer exists," anchor Malika Andrews said as her eyes welled up after that decision came down in 2022. "In less than 24 hours, we celebrated equal rights for women, and now we react to women's reproductive rights being taken away."

This political speech was given on a show called (checks notes) *NBA Today*. Can I just get the Knicks-Celtics highlights please? If I wanted an unhinged political screed, I'd watch Rachel Maddow (when she shows up for work, anyway).

But ESPN still has some sane commentators, such as Sam Ponder. Here's what she had to say in April 2023 regarding the issue of men competing against women:

"This would take away so many opportunities for biological women and girls in sports," Ponder tweeted at the time. "It is a shame that we are needing to fight for the integrity of Title IX in 2023 and the reason it was needed in the first place."

Yet so few women are doing so, particularly college athletes, because of the fear that comes with losing a scholarship that is potentially worth hundreds of thousands of dollars per year.

So instead of other women in sports journalism echoing Ponder's pragmatic sentiment, she was actually met with vitriol. Again, for *standing up for fairness*.

Enter Nancy Armour of *USA Today*, who penned a lecture for the paper, accusing Ponder of being a bigot.

"If ESPN's Sam Ponder was truly concerned about women's sports, she's had ample opportunity in the last year to call out the inequities that actually do exist. She hasn't," wrote Armour. "This isn't about 'fairness.' It's about her bigotry."

So Armour's argument is that the inequities of biological males racing against females simply do not exist? Lia Thomas was literally nominated to be 2022's Athlete of the Year! There are dozens upon dozens of examples of men racing against women. But here's Armour accusing Ponder of being a bigot?

The world has truly gone mad. Just take what happened to Oakland A's broadcaster Glen Kuiper in May during a pregame review of what he and his broadcast partner, Dallas Braden, did that day leading up to the game.

"We had a phenomenal day. [N-word] league museum. And Arthur Bryant's Barbeque," he said near the top of the NBC Sports San Francisco broadcast.

Kuiper, of course, meant to say "*Negro* Leagues Museum."

"A little bit earlier in the show, I said something, didn't come out quite the way I wanted it to," Kuiper said in an apology during the game. "I just wanted to apologize if it sounded different than I meant it to be said. I just wanted to apologize for that."

Kuiper was fired anyway. Can you imagine this? He had been the team's play-by-play guy for *seventeen years*. Never once, whether that be on the air or on social media, did he ever once sniff anything deemed controversial. It was live TV. A word came out wrong. And the fact that Kuiper had earlier visited the Negro Leagues Baseball Museum shows we're not dealing with the sports broadcasting version of David Duke.

If NBC had suspended him for a few games to avoid any PR fallout, that would have been understandable. But instead, Kuiper may never work in sports television again.

It seemingly never stops: tune in to ESPN other times, and you'll hear pundits calling players refusing for religious reasons to wear pride flags on their uniforms bigoted.

"That religious exemption BS is used in sports and otherwise also allows for people to be denied health care, jobs, apartments, children, prescriptions, all sorts of rights," ESPN panelist Sarah Spain declared on *Around the Horn* in the summer of 2022 after some members of the Tampa Bay Rays refused to wear pride flags on their uniforms, citing their religious beliefs.

"They're trying to use religious exemptions to affect the opportunities, services, available resources for people who are LGBTQ+," Spain argued, before accusing the Rays players in question of being "bigoted" for opposing wearing the pride flags.

Ugliness can be fixed. Wokeness is forever. Because in Ms. Spain's world, you must force people to do things against what their core values say they shouldn't. I mean, really . . . should professional sports players be shamed into wearing symbols or patches that they may disagree with on faith-based grounds? Of course not. There's nothing in the values of freedom of speech that says one has to conform to whatever your employer says you should conform to.

Six players on Tampa Bay, however, refused to wear the logos. Those players included Jason Adam, Jalen Beeks, Brooks Raley, Jeffrey Springs, and Ryan Thompson.

"It's a hard decision," Rays pitcher Jason Adam said when asked his choice by the *Tampa Bay Times*. "Because ultimately we all said what we want is them to know that all are welcome and loved here. But when we put it on our bodies, I think a lot of guys decided that it's just a lifestyle that maybe—not that they look down on anybody or think differently—it's just that maybe we don't want to encourage it if we believe in Jesus, who's encouraged us to live a lifestyle that would abstain from that behavior, just like [Jesus] encourages me as a heterosexual male to abstain from sex outside of the confines of marriage. It's no different."

To St. Louis Cardinals pitcher Jack Flaherty, this decision by some of the Rays players was deemed unacceptable.

"Absolute joke," he tweeted to his followers.

The criticism from Flaherty is noteworthy because Flaherty's first item on his Twitter bio is Philippians 4:13, which is a passage in the Bible. The twenty-six-year-old attended Catholic School from kindergarten until eighth grade and often talks about his faith and the role it plays in his life.

"That relationship with the Lord is the biggest part, and continuing to develop that relationship and just understanding different things about it and that the Lord is with you every step of the way," he told the *Table Forty* podcast hosted by the Cards' Matt Holliday and his wife, Leslee. "Even if you may come off that path and you find your way back to the Lord, He's going to be there with you. That relationship is something that continues to build and continues to grow and continues to change."

So it's surprising that Flaherty takes issue with several Rays players citing their religious beliefs for not agreeing to wear the pride logo. It should be noted that none of Tampa's players said anything derogatory about the gay community when talking about their choice. Adam even said that, regardless of sexual orientation, "all are loved and welcome here."

Let's put it this way: let's say during the Rays' next home stand that the team asked its players to wear an NRA patch to show they support the Second Amendment and the right to keep and bear arms. And let's say some players disagreed and refused to wear the logo. Would that be called a joke too?

Recent polls shows 70 percent of US voters on average support gay marriage. Count me among that 70 percent. To be blunt, I really don't care about anyone's sex life or who they date or marry regardless of gender. It's none of my business.

But also count me among those who believe that if a player or any individual doesn't want to wear a patch representing something they fundamentally disagree with, particularly due to religious reasons, they should have the right to opt out.

Jack Flaherty believes strongly in God and is led by his teachings in the Bible. Good for him.

"Do not judge, or you too will be judged," the Bible says in Matthew 7:1–3. "For in the same way you judge others, you will be judged, and with the measure you use, it will be measured to you. Why do you look at the speck of sawdust in your brother's eye and pay no attention to the plank in your own eye?"

The Cardinals pitcher might want to brush up on that part.

It got worse one evening during the 2022 NCAA Women's Basketball Tournament, when ESPN's Carolyn Peck and Courtney Lyle held a long moment of silence in response to Florida's parental rights bill that our corrupt media continually and inaccurately refers to as the "Don't Say Gay" bill.

"Normally at this time we would take a look back at the first half, but there are things that are bigger than basketball that need to be addressed at this time. Our friends, our family, our coworkers, the players and coaches in our community, are hurting right now," Lyle told viewers during halftime at the South Carolina and Richmond game. "Our LGBTQIA+ teammates at Disney asked for our solidarity and support, including our company's support, in opposition to the Parental Rights in Education Bill in the state of Florida, and similar legislation across the United States," Lyle continued. Disney owns ESPN, by the way.

"The threat to any rights is a threat to all human rights, and at this time, Courtney and I are going to take a pause from our broadcast to show our love and support for our friends, our families, and our colleagues," Peck added. The pair then went silent for two minutes as a play was happening. And their bosses took no issue with it.

What do you think would happen if two pro-life female announcers decided to hijack a broadcast to hold a two-minute moment of silence to honor the hundreds of thousands of babies aborted each year? How quickly would ESPN have them suspended or fired? Five minutes after the broadcast? Ten?

And by the way, how utterly dishonest Peck and Lyle were here. And to be so pious in the process is the icing on the cake. Let's unpack this, shall we?

DeSantis's blowout reelection over Charlie Crist in November 2022 included winning in heavily blue Miami-Dade and Palm Beach Counties. And the blowout came despite exceedingly negative media coverage on the local and national level, especially around the governor's Parental Rights in Education Bill, which prohibits teaching elementary school kids as young as pre-kindergarten about sexual orientation and gender identification.

On cue, very few outlets referred to the Parental Rights in Education Bill as such, instead taking their cues from Democratic activists and lawmakers who called it the "Don't Say Gay" Bill instead. The word *gay* isn't mentioned in the bill *once*, but the media ran with it anyway in an effort to smear DeSantis and dupe ESPN announcers.

Associated Press: *"'Don't Say Gay' Bill Signed by Florida Gov. Ron DeSantis"*

Washington Post: *"What Is Florida's 'Don't Say Gay' Bill?"*

NBC News: *"What Florida's 'Don't Say Gay' Bill Actually Says"*

There are dozens of other examples, but you get the point. The media was going to simply rename this bill in lockstep. And since a growing number of people only read headlines on social media and maybe a short caption below it, they jump to improper conclusions, like "OMG! Ron DeSantis just banned the word 'gay' in Florida public schools and put LGBTQ persons at risk! This is an attack on human rights that shall not stand!"

DeSantis, for his part, was having none of it when a reporter referred to it as "Don't Say Gay" during a press conference in the spring of 2022. "The idea that you wouldn't be honest about that and tell people what it actually says, it's why people don't trust people like you, because you peddle false narratives, and so we disabuse you of those narratives," the governor said, drawing applause from nonreporters in the room. "We're going to make sure that parents can send their kid to kindergarten without having some of this stuff injected into the school curriculum."

In a related story, polls showed after the bill was passed that more than *60 percent* of Floridians approved of the language in the bill.

Wow, that's *a lot* of anti-LGBTQ people who support this threat to human rights. Or maybe, *just maybe*, normal parents of all political stripes simply do not want their young children being taught this crap.

Of course, it's not like ESPN has zero right-leaning voices on its roster. Take Sage Steele, who said this to former Chicago Bears quarterback Jay Cutler on his podcast around Disney's mandate to have all ESPN employees vaccinated. So much for her body, her choice.

"I respect everyone's decision, I really do, but to mandate it is sick and it's scary to me in many ways. I just, I'm not surprised it got to this point, especially with Disney, I mean a global company like that," she told Cutler.

The biracial Steele also commented on the US Census asking to check off a race.

"If they make [me] choose a race, I go, 'both,'" she said. "Barack Obama chose Black and he's biracial. And I'm like, 'Congratulations to the president. That's his thing.' I think that's fascinating considering his Black dad was nowhere to be found and his white mom and grandma raised him, but hey, you do you. I'm gonna do me."

For ESPN, this is *way* over the line. Call Donald Trump a "white supremacist," as then *SportsCenter* anchor Jemele Hill did? Hey, no problem! Simply wonder aloud why Barack Obama considers himself Black and not biracial despite his upbringing, *that's* gonna cost you.

Steele, a sixteen-year veteran of the network, filed a lawsuit against ESPN and Disney for retaliating against her by pulling assignments, all for exercising her free speech rights. On August 15, 2023, the suit was finally settled. Steele was finally free. And then she really teed off.

"All I ever wanted was consistency," Steele told Megyn Kelly on her podcast after she left the network. "And if we are allowing my peers to go on social media, much less on our own airwaves, saying things . . . that have nothing to do with sports that are political, . . . then I should be allowed on my personal time to give my opinion on my experiences personally, without telling others what to do. . . . I think that's just what breaks my heart. That there were different rules for me than everyone else."

Easy rule here: *always* follow the money in these situations. And when social media howls got louder about sports and the escapism being robbed from viewers, ESPN management finally had to at least try to put a stop to it.

"ESPN is a journalistic organization—not a political organization. We should do nothing to undermine that position," ESPN senior vice president Kevin Merida told staffers in 2017 during an internal meeting. "ESPN's focus is sports. By-and-large we are not experts on politics, healthcare policies, terrorism, commerce—that's not what we do."

That sentiment, unfortunately, didn't hold up.

Go woke, go broke.

American corporations are quickly learning this lesson.

"Sports journalists" should take note.

Despite all of this political correctness and moral preening turning more Americans off to the party and its supporters across media, it still is good to be a Democrat in 2024. Just ask President Biden. . . .

CHAPTER 22

Not Your Daddy's *60 Minutes*

The most successful broadcast news magazine in history celebrated the opening of its fifty-fifth season on Sunday night by landing an interview with President Biden in the fall of 2022. The get was a fairly big deal for *60 Minutes*, considering Biden had been hiding from such interviews in recent months, with the president's last sit-down occurring on Super Bowl Sunday on February 10 of that year, more than 220 days prior.

But for those who are nostalgic for the good ole days of *60 Minutes* being one of the tougher Q&As anyone in power can face during the tenure of Mike Wallace, the rhetorical foot massage provided by correspondent Scott Pelley might as well have been conducted by Jen Psaki at her new home, MSNBC.

The introduction set the tone for the pretaped package:

"Summer was going so well for the President, the White House threw a party last week with a concert by James Taylor. Mr. Biden's streak began in June when he signed a bipartisan gun safety law. Then in August, over Republican objections, he signed the largest investment ever on climate change, a minimum tax on corporations, a law to lower prescription drug prices, and student loan forgiveness."

Hey, what was the largest investment ever on climate change and the law to lower prescription drug prices again? It has a name. Ah, right:

the Inflation Reduction Act. Surely Pelley will cite study after study showing the act wasn't going to reduce inflation, right? Given that the interview—like all Biden interviews—was pretaped days before its airing on Sunday night to allow for editing and to avoid Biden embarrassing himself on live TV, surely there would be plenty of time for *60 Minutes* producers to research and include that rather sizable tidbit.

That moment never came.

Instead, the president (again) lied to the American people, claiming the bill had already "lowered costs for families at the kitchen table" (it was quite the opposite, per the Consumer Price Index at the time). OK, so how about student loan forgiveness, which Pelley also touted? Well, there was yet another an opportunity to bring that up after Biden declared the pandemic was "over."

What does student loan forgiveness have to do with the pandemic? As columnist Charles W. Cooke noted:

"Why does Biden's statement matter so much? I'll tell you: It matters because the memo that the Biden administration released to justify his [student loan forgiveness] order rested entirely upon there being an ongoing emergency, and because, as Biden has just confirmed, there is no ongoing emergency."

That's correct. Biden was only able to unilaterally sign student loan forgiveness under the 2003 HEROES act, which was designed to assist borrower servicing in the US military after the 9/11 attacks two years earlier. The president's legal team argued that student loan forgiveness should fall under HEROES because the pandemic was an ongoing national emergency. By Biden's own admission, that was all BS in an effort to buy votes. Pelley and his producing team failed to mention that as well.

Here was another doozy of a question:

"With the Federal Reserve rapidly raising interest rates, what can you do to prevent a recession?" Pelley asked.

Prevent a recession? According to the traditional definition of two straight quarters of negative growth, the US was already in a recession at that time. Biden and his administration have insisted that's not the case. So Pelley simply echoed the home team narrative instead of framing it in a negative (and proper) way.

Later in the interview, Pelley did note that the president's approval rating was well below 50 percent but then somehow allowed the president to tout vaccination numbers: "When I got in office, when I got elected, only 2 million people had been vaccinated," Biden said. "I got 220 million—my point is it takes time. We were left in a very difficult situation. It's been a very difficult time, very difficult."

Pelley offered no pushback. Gee, why were only 2 million people vaccinated when Biden took office? Maybe it was because, I don't know . . . the vaccine had barely been on the market at that point!

Context also would have been nice here, because when Biden took office, his approval was well above 50 percent. In other words, Covid had almost nothing to do with Biden poll numbers being so low; they were low because of inflation due to reckless spending, spiking violent crime, the border being anything but secure, and the issue that started the plunge: the incompetent withdrawal of US forces from Afghanistan more than one year before.

"Republicans are most likely to go after your son Hunter once again," Pelley warned at another part of the interview.

Funny how the correspondent framed that, going into full "Republicans pounce" mode. To review, it was *60 Minutes* and Lesley Stahl who insisted shortly before the 2020 election that the contents of Hunter Biden's laptop could not be verified, therefore not making it worth their time to investigate.

"This is the most important issue in the country right now?" Stahl condescendingly asked Trump when he broached Hunter's laptop.

"It's a very important issue to find out whether a man's corrupt who's running for president, who's accepted money from China, and Ukraine, and from Russia," Trump replied. "Take a look at what's going on, Lesley, and you say that shouldn't be discussed? I think it's one of the biggest scandals I've ever seen, and you don't cover it."

"Well, because it can't be verified," Stahl retorted. "I'm telling you—"

"Of course it can be verified," Trump countered. "Excuse me, Lesley, they found a laptop."

"It can't be verified," Stahl repeated, chuckling.

It couldn't be verified, Lesley, because investigative shows like *60 Minutes* never bothered to use their vast resources to verify it like they might have in the past.

Instead, most of the media relied on fifty-one former intelligence officials, many proven to be partisan actors on cable news, to declare in an open letter that Hunter Biden's laptop and its contents were the product of Russian disinformation. Their reasoning appeared to point to the timing of the laptop and its contents being exposed (weeks before the election) and was basically based on a hunch.

"Such an operation would be consistent with Russian objectives, as outlined publicly and recently by the Intelligence Community, to create political chaos in the United States and to deepen political divisions here but also to undermine the candidacy of former Vice President Biden and thereby help the candidacy of President Trump," the letter reads.

Signatories of said letter included anti-Trump former intelligence officials John Brennan (former CIA director, current NBC/MSNBC national security analyst), James Clapper (former director of national intelligence, current CNN analyst), and Jeremy Bash (former CIA chief of staff, current MSNBC analyst), along with forty-eight others.

So did these former intelligence officers have proof to back up their claim?

Of course not.

"We do not know if the emails, provided to the *New York Post* by President Trump's personal attorney Rudy Giuliani, are genuine or not and that we do not have evidence of Russian involvement," the letter provided to *Politico* adds. "Just that our experience makes us deeply suspicious that the Russian government played a significant role in this case.

"If we are right, this is Russia trying to influence how Americans vote in this election, and we believe strongly that Americans need to be aware of this," the letter states.

So to unpack this in retrospect, these former intel heads admit they did not "have evidence of Russian involvement," but all were in total agreement because of their suspicions from afar? And like seagulls at the beach, a solid majority of the press blindly swallowed the narrative whole.

We heard a lot about collusion during the Trump era, but the real collusion happened between broadcast print and social media, all working together to either squash or dismiss the Hunter Biden laptop story.

Twitter and Facebook handled the squashing part, with the former locking the accounts of anyone who even shared the *New York Post* story in October 2020. The *Post*'s own account was locked, as was then White House press secretary Kayleigh McEnany's and the official handle of the Trump campaign. Again, these Pyongyang tactics all occurred just a few weeks before a presidential election.

Facebook also pointed to "the spread of misinformation" as a reason to "reduce distribution" of the story.

"While I will intentionally not link to the *New York Post*, I want to be clear that this story is eligible to be fact checked by Facebook's third-party fact checking partners. In the meantime, we are reducing its distribution on our platform," wrote Andy Stone, Facebook's communications policy manager on October 14, 2020. "This is part of our standard process to reduce the spread of misinformation. We temporarily reduce distribution pending fact-checker review."

It should be noted that before Stone became a powerful Facebook executive, he worked for the Democrats' House Majority PAC, then senator Barbara Boxer (D-CA), the Democratic Congressional Campaign Committee, and Rep. Jerry McNerney (D-CA).

Since dismissing it before the 2020 election, the *Washington Post* and the *New York Times* have since confirmed the *New York Post*'s original reporting that the laptop belongs to the president's son and the contents were real. And instead of Pelley pressing the president on emails show-ing influence-peddling in Ukraine and China and someone nicknamed "the big guy" receiving 10 percent of profits (Hunter's business partner, Tony Bobulinski, insists the big guy is Joe Biden), he simply allowed the president to skate by with this answer:

"There's not a single thing that I've observed at all from that that would affect me or the United States relative to my son Hunter," Biden claimed. "We've also reduced the debt and reduced the deficit by $350 billion my first year. This year, it's going to be over $1.5 trillion [that we've] reduced the debt."

Again, producers and Pelley had time to fact-check such a farcical claim in the post-edit. That fact-check never came. So I guess I have to handle this: federal spending rose by about 45 percent in the year Biden was referring to (2021), according to the CBO. That maybe took me ninety seconds to fact-check.

But nothing resembling a basic follow-up challenge came from Pelley, who then proceeded to end the interview with these lines right out of an Aaron Sorkin *West Wing* script.

"You have lived a long life of triumph and tragedy. In November, you'll be 80. And I wonder what it is that keeps you in the arena," he cooed.

If you're having trouble envisioning a Republican in power, say . . . Governor Ron DeSantis or Glenn Youngkin, receiving that kind of air kiss, you're not alone.

The Biden White House communications team must have been thrilled that so many narratives they've been pushing got a seal of ap-proval and boost from *60 Minutes*, which clearly isn't your father's *60 Minutes* anymore.

We also know that this program has largely become a joke based on their hires in recent years, most notably Anderson Cooper. So here's some trivia: What was the most-watched *60 Minutes* episode in the past ten years?

If you somehow guessed the March 25, 2018, episode that featured the beacon of truth that is the creepy Michael Avenatti and feminine icon/ adult film star Stormy Daniels, you are correct! And it was Cooper who conducted this "interview" of a Trump-bashing session right out of the CNN playbook (Avenatti, by the way, is currently serving a federal sentence for tax fraud and cheating his clients out of money, while Stormy has been ordered to pay more than $600,000 after losing a defamation suit against the former president).

60 Minutes still has considerable sway. It's almost always a top-ten program on television. But the days of conservatives and liberals and independents tuning in are long gone. Much like *Time* or *Rolling Stone* or CNN, this is a show that caters to the donkey party.

And that's not just an opinion. And it's not just confined to CBS. For example, in the 2008 election, CBS employees, along with those employed by ABC and NBC, donated $1,020,816 to the Democratic Party, according to an analysis by the *Washington Examiner* and the Center for Responsive Politics. So how much was donated to the Republican Party? Just $142,863.

Pew Research also dug into who's watching, from a political perspective. Regarding CBS, once the crown jewel of broadcast journalism and the longtime home of Walter Cronkite, 40 percent of its news audience holds political views from the left or left of center, while just 20 percent of its news audience consider themselves right or right of center.

It wasn't long ago that *60 Minutes* seemed to care about its reputation and credibility.

We all remember the hit piece that ran shortly before the 2004 presidential election (George W. Bush versus John Kerry), when Dan Rather dropped a huge bombshell around Bush's military service or, according to Rather, lack thereof.

With the close election ultimately coming down to the state of Ohio, a *60 Minutes* piece stating that a sitting commander in chief lied about his military service could have resulted in a President Kerry. But it was quickly discovered that the whole foundation of the Rather and Mapes report on Bush was based on documents proven to be fabricated because the font they used hadn't existed at the time they were supposedly written.

Both Rather and Mapes were forced to resign not long thereafter. Ironically, Rather would go on to be a regular guest on Brian Stelter's *Reliable Sources* on CNN to talk about media ethics.

Sometimes the jokes really do write themselves.

Speaking of jokes, Kamala Harris, who almost never does TV interviews, was featured on *60 Minutes* in October 2023 while she was polling lower than any VP in polling history. But here's the treatment she got from correspondent Bill Whitaker:

"She showed us around the vice president's ceremonial office," narrated Whitaker in what felt more like an edition of MTV's *Cribs*. "She showed us the desk where previous vice presidents left their signatures."

"There's Al Gore, Quayle, Cheney, Harry Truman," Harris said, pointing at the signatures.

"Some of these men went on to become president," Whitaker noted. "But Kamala Harris told us she is focused on getting the Biden-Harris ticket reelected next year. The GOP is using her low poll numbers and President Biden's age as a battering ram, and some Democrats are growing worried."

Per a 2022 CNN poll and others, more than seven in ten Americans believe that Joe Biden should not seek a second term and cite his age as their top reason, so it's unclear why Whitaker was framing this as a "GOP pounces" moment.* Even an overwhelming majority of Democrats didn't want the president to run again.

"The Biden-Harris ticket is running neck and neck with Donald Trump," Whitaker later noted. "Why are you not 30 points ahead?"

"Well, I'm not—I'm not a political pundit, so I—I—I'm not gonna

---

* Kate Sullivan, "CNN Poll: 75% of Democratic Voters Want Someone Other Than Biden in 2024," CNN, July 27, 2022, https://edition.cnn.com/2022/07/26/politics /cnn-poll-biden-2024/index.html; Caroline Vakil, "71 Percent Don't Want Biden to Run for Reelection: Poll," *The Hill*, July 1, 2022, https://thehill.com/homenews /campaign/3543867-71-percent-dont-want-biden-to-run-for-reelection-poll/.

speak to that," Harris responded, per the official CBS transcript. "But what I will say is this: When the American people are able to take a close look at election time on their options, I think the choice is gonna be clear. Bill, we're gonna win. Let me just tell you that. We're gonna win. And I'm not saying it's gonna be easy. But we will win."

"You say that with such conviction," Whitaker oozed in response.

But the most frustrating part about watching this interview was what Whitaker allowed Harris to get away with when it came to discussing the crisis that is a catastrophe at the southern US border.

"The number of people trying to cross the U.S. southern border is—at an all-time high," Whitaker noted without sharing just how high that number is (2.47 million apprehended in the 2023 fiscal year alone), or any context compared to past administrations.

"It's no secret that we have a broken immigration system," Harris responded, echoing Biden's generic excuse. "Short term, we need a safe, orderly, and humane border policy. And long term, we need to invest in the root causes of migration. But the bottom line? Congress needs to act. Come on. Participate in the solution instead of political gamesmanship."

Whitaker simply moved on without any pushback, which should have included the fact that Congress acted back in May, passing the Secure the Border Act in the lower chamber, before it stalled in the Democrat-controlled Senate. The bill calls for resuming border wall construction, increasing the number of Border Patrol agents, tightening asylum standards, and requiring employers to e-verify.

It is interesting that one of the few places Joe Biden and Kamala Harris have granted broadcast interviews to recently has been *60 Minutes*. But when you get this kind of PR from its team, it's easy to see why the usually media-averse administration has been running there.

More from Whitaker:

"If politics is a game, Kamala Harris has proven herself to be a savvy player, forging a career that has gone from one first to another," Whitaker said, as various photos of Harris being sworn in were shown onscreen. "The child of an Indian mother and a Jamaican father, she was the first woman district attorney for San Francisco; the first woman to serve as California's attorney general; the first woman of color elected senator from California. And the first woman and woman of color to be elected vice president of the United States."

You can go barf now.

60 Minutes used to speak truth to power. It still speaks, but just as the PR arm for a Democratic Party that is becoming more and more like the "news channel" with a clunky acronym dubiously featured in our next chapter.

CHAPTER 23

Not Your Daddy's MSNBC

The pushback against the cable news network from liberal organizations was growing more fierce by the day. Thousands of signatures were gathered by the Gay and Lesbian Alliance Against Defamation, for example, saying the news channel launched in 1996 simply had gone too far to the right.

Lest anyone think we're talking about Fox News, this chapter is about MSNBC.

MSNBC of the pre-Obama era contrasts with the MSNBC of today. And as a guy who has covered media and politics for more than a decade, from Mediaite to *The Hill* to the *Messenger* and obviously on Fox News, let's just say researching the material for this chapter has been an absolute blast.

Take, for example, this completely accurate 2003 *Washington Post* story by Howie Kurtz, who covered media for the publication at the time while hosting CNN's *Reliable Sources*—before the show's name became a punch line in the Stelter era.

"Some media critics say the network, which has a news alliance with the *Washington Post*, is lurching to the right in an effort to compete with top-rated Fox News Channel," Kurtz reported after MSNBC announced it was awarding a program to (checks notes) Michael Savage.

Yes, *that* Michael Savage. The same Savage that called MSNBC

"More Snotty Nonsense By Creeps" and referred to then MSNBC reporter Ashleigh Banfield—a nice, intelligent person—as "the mind-slut with a big pair of glasses that they sent to Afghanistan," per Kurtz's story.

And Savage wasn't a one-off from the right. Tucker Carlson (yes, that Tucker Carlson) also had a show on the network. Pat Buchanan was part of the team. So was Alan Keyes. And remember Jesse Ventura, the WWE wrestler turned Republican Minnesota governor? Even *that guy* got his own show.

"We're a big tent that encourages perspectives from all ends of the ideological spectrum," an MSNBC spokesperson said at the time.

But ratings didn't follow, thereby collapsing that big tent.

The keys to the network were instead handed over to Keith Olbermann, the former ESPN *SportsCenter* cohost who, along with Dan Patrick, helped turn a sports highlight show into a cultural phenomenon.

I remember going on Keith's show in 2003 to talk about a big controversy regarding the University of Colorado's football program. There have been only three times I've ever been nervous going on television: for my first field report on a community access show I worked on (for free, of course) called *Rock & Roll TV*, in high school on WCEP-TV, and when going on *Countdown with Keith Olbermann* in March 2003.

Olbermann was someone I had idolized. I taped *SportsCenter* every weekday night and watched it religiously. I was working in sports at the time, having first started out as a weekend freelance producer for Time Warner's NY-1 on a live local sports program called *Sports on 1* that aired every night at 11:30 p.m.

And when I say "producer," it should be noted that I was the *only* producer to put together the show on Saturday and Sunday nights. That meant logging highlights from any one of New York's nine area professional sports teams, editing those highlights as well as sound from postgame press conferences and locker room interviews, bringing the tapes down to the control room, organizing them, and even hitting the play button when the anchor was ready to narrate them. There was also the matter of putting together the rundown for the show, booking guests, and screening phone calls on the fly. So when I tell you this was easily the most difficult but most educational and satisfying job I've ever had, that's no exaggeration.

Fortunately, I was surrounded by pros, including anchors Steve Cangialosi (who went on to be a great play-by-play guy for the New Jersey Devils and New York Red Bulls), the affable Budd Mishkin, and fellow Jerseyan Kevin Geraghty, who would go on to do fine work with NY-1 for more than twenty-five years during a time when New York teams actually won championships. All three men were always willing to help put the show together, as was my executive producer, Mark Weingarten, who always seemed to have a smile on his face despite long hours. Anyone who has worked at NY-1 will tell you: We're all grinders regardless of title or rank.

On the nights I wasn't working, I watched both *Sports on 1* and *SportsCenter*, the latter of which was like watching Tiger Woods if looking to improve one's golf swing. I always marveled at the seamless humor and chemistry Olbermann and Patrick had, as well as the pace of the show. So when Keith began getting into trouble with management in 1997 after criticizing ESPN (once calling it a "Godforsaken place," which led to a suspension), I couldn't understand why he would screw up what looked like the best job in sports. Olbermann would bolt the network in late 1997 and, after a stint at Fox Sports, oddly went to MSNBC, who gave him the coveted 8:00 p.m. spot in 2003.

The show's ratings were average in Olbermann's first year, but that quickly changed after his screed against George W. Bush over the Iraq War, which went viral among the left at a time before Twitter or YouTube even existed.

"How dare you, Mr. President, after taking cynical advantage of the unanimity and love, and transmuting it into fraudulent war and needless death, after monstrously transforming it into fear and suspicion and turning that fear into the campaign slogan of three elections? How dare you—or those around you—ever 'spin' 9/11?" Olbermann said in what he dubbed his "Special Comment," with Ground Zero as a backdrop.

"Who has left this hole in the ground? We have not forgotten, Mr. President. You have. May this country forgive you," he concluded.

But it was the wake of the 2004 election that really propelled Olbermann as a go-to voice for Democrats. If you recall, George W. Bush won reelection by the skin of his teeth; if Ohio had gone to John Kerry, we would have witnessed another Bush serve as just a one-term president.

But Olbermann was convinced that nefarious things happened in Ohio to give Bush the victory. And if any of this sounds familiar to you, as if it came not from Olbermann in 2004 but Sidney Powell or Rudy Giuliani in 2020, it should.

Olbermann, November 8, 2004, MSNBC:

> Democrats and critics of our Rube Goldberg election processes say that it is an extraordinary coincidence that all the reports of voting machines going crazy turn out with the machines giving votes to Mr. Bush or subtracting them from Senator Kerry.

Voting machines giving votes to one candidate and subtracting from the other? Who would ever make such a claim?

Olbermann, in 2004, during an interview with Rep. John Conyers (D-MI), MSNBC:

> **Conyers:** *"Well, I'm glad you're investigating this because it's very central to the whole idea that everybody's vote counts. And these irregularities are sufficient in number, and more and more members are joining me every day on this."*

> **Olbermann:** *"You can choose your terminology, sir, I wouldn't put it, especially after what you've just said, I wouldn't put any words in your mouth, but is it your assessment that last Tuesday's election was, to some*

*degree, invalid, hacked, rigged, fixed, otherwise flawed, and what do you
want done about the previous election as opposed to future elections?"*

Conyers: *"I can't tell you yes or no because I haven't had the
investigation yet . . ."*

Fast-forward to the present day, and almost no day goes by without
Olbermann running to Twitter or declaring on his podcast that Donald
Trump is America's Hitler and that the former president should be
thrown in jail for the rest of his life for saying the election was stolen.*
Will Keith be his cellmate for asking a sitting congressman in 2004 if
that presidential election was "invalid, hacked, rigged, fixed, otherwise
flawed?"

For the rest of that decade, MSNBC's prime-time ratings went up
almost across the board. And by the 2008 presidential campaign, it
moved from third to second place, surpassing CNN. Its audience had
more than doubled from the 2004 campaign season. Almost all of its
conservative hosts were purged as a result of the ratings growth. And
its most credible anchor, the legendary Tim Russert, suddenly passed
away in 2008, leaving MSNBC with no host of real stature to actually
report the news objectively and challenge both political parties. Instead, Olbermann was named a coanchor on election night, along with
former Carter speechwriter Chris Matthews and David Gregory, the
guy who replaced Russert on *Meet the Press*, only to fail so badly that he
was replaced by Chuck Todd after a few forgettable years.

Shortly before the 2008 election, Olbermann's favorite guest, Rachel
Maddow, was awarded her own prime-time program to follow his at
9:00 p.m. in September 2008 . . . just two months before Barack Obama
became the nation's first Black president, beating the moderate GOP
nominee and war hero John McCain.

---

* Keith Olbermann, "The Media Just Figured It Out: Trump Is Hitler," YouTube
  video, November 14, 2023, https://www.youtube.com/watch?v=7o1JPSYrnyk.

But, hey—Olbermann wouldn't go after McCain too harshly, right? Think again. Because Obama was MSNBC's new god, his opponent not only defeated but humiliated.

August 18, 2008: Olbermann's conclusion to a "Special Comment" monologue where he refers to McCain as a "jackass": "Let's have an adult campaign here, in other words, and I am embarrassed to have to say this to a man who turns 72 at the end of this month: Senator, grow up!"

MSNBC would never look back. In 2012, with Obama facing another moderate nice guy in Massachusetts governor Mitt Romney, the coverage was astonishingly and embarrassingly biased. Pew Research found that of the fifty-one stories MSNBC did on Obama in the campaign's final week, all fifty-one were positive, while all sixty-eight stories it did on Romney were negative.[*]

But Olbermann's star at MSNBC was starting to fade. Ironically, Maddow's audience and influence among the left began eclipsing his. He also made the mistake so many in this business make: believing that he was untouchable. Indispensable. Bigger than the network itself. And on November 5, 2020, after it was revealed he had donated the maximum allowed to three Democratic candidates, violating MSNBC policy, the network suspended him. And two months after that suspension, KO was abruptly KO'd. The host and network say they simply "parted ways."

Olbermann would go on to host a show on the Al Gore and Al Jazeera–owned Current TV, which looked very much like my old set in high school on *Rock & Roll TV*. Maddow was the face now, and she used her platform to tell her audience these whoppers:

Maddow on the Covid vaccine:

"A vaccinated person gets exposed to the virus, the virus does not infect them, the virus cannot then use that person to go anywhere else.

---

* "Final Weeks in the Mainstream Press," Pew Research Center, November 16, 2012, https://www.pewresearch.org/journalism/2012/11/16/final-weeks-mainstream-press/.

"Now we know that the vaccines work well enough that the virus stops with every vaccinated person. . . . The virus does not infect them. . . . It cannot use a vaccinated person as a host to get more people."

Heh.

Maddow on Trump being a spy for Russia, 2018:

"The basic question, which I think rung so loud for everybody in the country this week was, is our president subordinate to a foreign power? Does our president answer to a foreign government and a foreign leader? And that private meeting with Putin, where nobody knows what he promised or what he may have given away, the way that he responded to Putin when we saw him face-to-face, and then the fact that he took under consideration all of these demands from Russia, including handing over Americans to Russia for interrogation. That just—you know, it makes the worst-case scenario really palpable. The worst-case scenario that the president is a foreign agent suddenly feels very palpable."

That wasn't an isolated comment, either. It was practically every night during Maddow's never-ending monologues. *The Intercept* did a great analysis on what Maddow was feeding her viewers as MSNBC's number one host. During one six-week period in 2017, they found that 53 percent of her broadcast time was dedicated to Trump and Russia. Fifty-three percent on a story that ended up being a figment of her imagination.

MSNBC brass was also wise enough to grant professional race-baiter Joy Reid her own prime-time show. This is the same Joy Reid who wrote profoundly homophobic and anti-Semitic content on her blog more than a decade ago, only to blame hackers for changing the content (which would be impossible without access to a time-traveling DeLorean and 1.21 gigawatts). She would later apologize to the LGBTQ community, but not for making the whole thing up. Apparently, that gets you promoted at MSNBC, which moved her weekend show to 7:00 p.m. weeknights anyway while also giving her Olbermann's old job of being an election night coanchor.

"As a teenager living in New York, I've said it before, this is why I never watched *The Apprentice*. I despised Donald Trump. He signified the rich white guy in Manhattan that absolutely hated and despised me," Reid declared on the air in August 2023.

This kind of stuff really is too easy to fact-check:

Joy Reid is approaching age sixty.

The Apprentice aired when she was in her thirties and forties.

She was raised in Colorado until she was seventeen, when she moved to Brooklyn.

She attended Harvard undergrad shortly thereafter.

Her net worth is reportedly $4 million.

But, hey, besides that, everything she said sounds totally true!

The 2023 version of MSNBC is the very thing it warns its viewers about. It is very much against the free exchange of speech and ideas. It is next to impossible to find any Republicans except for the Nicolle Wallace version. Wallace, who according to Pulitzer-winning journalist Glenn Greenwald is "the Typhoid Mary of disinformation," is a former communications director for President George W. Bush who has declared definitively on MSNBC that . . .

- Hunter Biden's laptop is the product of a Russian disinformation campaign.
- Covid coming from a lab in Wuhan is a conspiracy theory being pushed by Trump.
- Capitol Police officer Brian Sicknick was "murdered" after being "beaten to death" on January 6.
- The Steele dossier "may be dirty but it ain't fake."
- Trump, while president, was "talking about exterminating Latinos."

I could go on and on, but we've got finite space here.

The other "Republican" on the network to serve as a host is Joe Scarborough, who actually left the party not long after Trump was inaugurated. But the irony is, Scarborough, along with cohost and wife Mika Brzezinski, are partially responsible for Trump's rise to the presidency.

Their interviews throughout the 2015–16 primary season were textbook examples of ass-kissing. Other MSNBCers didn't seem to mind, because they, like most of the media establishment, believed Trump had zero chance of winning and liked the ratings boost he provided on his way to a certain defeat in 2016.

Matt Taibbi's scathing piece in a February 2016 piece in *Rolling Stone* says it all:

MORNING BLOW: HOW JOE AND MIKA BECAME TRUMP'S LAPDOGS

Joe Scarborough and Mika Brzezinski should be herded into a rocket and shot into space for their brown-nosing of Trump.

Taibbi goes on to highlight one exchange between the three old friends. From the *Rolling Stone* piece:

"You know what I thought was kind of a wow moment, was the guy you brought up on stage," Mika says to Trump.

"We played it several times this morning!" added a breathless Scarborough.

An approving Trump here verbally extends his ring to be kissed. "I watched your show this morning," he says. "You have me almost as a legendary figure, I like that."

Taibbi sums it up perfectly: "If any politician ever said that to me, I would eat a cyanide capsule on the spot."

Once Trump actually captured the nomination in April 2016 and the criticism of *Morning Joe*'s fawning over Trump grew stronger, Joe and Mika did a complete one-eighty. And it got personal and reckless after Scarborough, with zero evidence, implied Trump had dementia in May 2016.

"My mother had dementia for 10 years," he said after playing a

Trump sound bite. "That sounds like the sort of thing my mother would say today . . . it's beyond the realm." In the same month, he called Trump a "bumbling, bumbling dope" who looked like "a kid who pooped in his pants."

And here's Scarborough in late 2023: Trump "will imprison, he will execute whoever he is allowed to imprison, execute, and drive from the country. Just look at his past. It's not really hard to read."

You read that right: a morning show host who used to be good buddies with Trump just said he will execute his political opponents. The same host says to look at Trump's record as president, which at last check didn't include any firing squads.

This has been the tone of the show every day for the past three-plus years since. *Morning Joe* actually used to be decent to watch and would attract members on both sides of the aisle in a conversational format. No more. Now it's just nonstop hate and lectures from the hosts on democracy and morality. *Phony* is the only word coming to mind regarding that sentiment. MSNBC used to be the home for everyone, from Tucker Carlson to Laura Ingraham to Ann Coulter to Chris Matthews to Phil Donohue to John Seigenthaler to Dan Abrams to Don Imus.

MSNBC ain't the 1996 or even the 2003 version of itself anymore. It's what Keith Olbermann always wanted it to be: an angry, uncivil entity that seeks to divide the country through one batshit-crazy prism.

CNN also used to be a much, much different network. One of gravitas and trust in the twentieth century.

But those days are also long gone, as are its viewers. Strap yourself in for a full chapter on the death of CNN, whose demise was self-induced, thanks to its unwavering service to today's Democratic Party.

CHAPTER 24

Mutiny at CNN Shows Why Objective Media Is Doomed

In May 2022, Chris Licht left as executive producer of *The Tonight Show with Stephen Colbert* to become the president of CNN. Given CNN's forty-plus-year history and the money offered to make the jump, it's hard to blame Licht, fifty-one at the time, for taking on the enormous task of fixing what was (and remains) a broken news network.

When Licht entered its New York headquarters, CNN was reeling. And we're not talking the usual 15 to 20 percent drops we see in post-election years; we're talking about *80 percent of the audience gone*. The drop was for several reasons: the once-trusted network had alienated conservatives and Republicans, as well as many independents and old-school Democrats, who appreciated the even-handed style of award-winning journalists like Bernard Shaw.

But this wasn't Shaw's network anymore—far from it. One study out of Harvard underscores this point perfectly: during Donald Trump's first hundred days in office, which is normally considered the honeymoon period for any presidency, CNN led all "news organizations" by covering Trump negatively 93 percent of the time. Anchors who once delivered the news without much opinion were suddenly performing soaring monologues about the danger Trump posed to the country and the world.

"Will you and your neighbors just shrug or will you demand more honesty from your government?" asked Brian Stelter during a monologue on his ironically titled media analysis program, *Reliable Sources*, just one day after Trump took office in 2017.

"Cheesy" is the best way to describe Stelter. As a media observer myself, I can honestly say there isn't a more awkward person to watch on television.

"And what about the media? Is Trump just trying to twist us into knots? Is it working? Or is there an end goal?" his BS questions continued, in the most melodramatic way imaginable.

Do Trump's allies want to silence skeptics in the media, destroy the press or maybe support an alternative press that presents an alternative reality that's more favorable? Will conservative media outlets play along with Trump's lies? Will they claim he is telling the truth or will conservative outlets respect their readers enough to call BS on BS?

And finally. What can all newsrooms do to help you know what's really going on? These are uncomfortable questions, especially these last ones, but it's time to ask them. Do citizens in dictatorships recognize what's happening right here right now? Are they looking at the first two days of the Trump administration and saying, "Oh, that's what my leader does?" What should we learn from them today?

Again, this screed was given on national television by someone claiming to be objective *just after* President Trump took office.

Stelter had barely said a word about the previous Obama-Biden administration regarding their dictator-like behavior toward the press. Here are a few facts you'll never hear BS share among his BS:

Fact: The Obama-Biden administration secretly seized phone records of reporters at the Associated Press.

Fact: The Obama-Biden administration rejected more FOIA (Freedom of Information Act) requests than any administration in history.

Fact: The Obama-Biden Justice Department, under Attorney General Eric Holder, unlawfully spied on James Rosen, Fox News correspondent at the time, calling him a flight risk.

There were no dramatic monologues around any of those items from Stelter as Team Obama left the White House. And it's this kind of omission that makes the formerly omnipotent senior media correspondent a ridiculous figure in the eyes of the sane and sober.

"You're full of sanctimony. You become part of one of the parts of the problem of the media," author Michael Wolff said directly to Stelter on his program in July 2021. "You know, you come on here and you have a monopoly on truth. You know exactly how things are supposed to be done. You are one of the reasons why people can't stand the media."

"You're cracking me up!" Stelter oddly replied before later asking, "Do you feel that my style is wrong, or my substance is wrong, trying to fact-check the president?"

"I mean this with truly no disrespect, but I think you can border on being sort of quite a ridiculous figure," Wolff responded. "It's not a good look to repeatedly and self-righteously defend your own self-interest."

Precisely. And when violent protests engulfed American cities in the summer of 2020, some CNN prime-time anchors and reporters actually defended the behavior, reporters on the ground claiming that the riots were "mostly peaceful" as buildings burned bright orange like the Nakatomi Plaza at the end of *Die Hard*.

"It says it right in the name: Antifa. Anti-fascism, which is what they were there fighting," former "anchor" Don Lemon explained in reference to the violent far-left organization.

"Listen, no organization is perfect," he continued. "There was some violence. No one condones violence, but there were different reasons for Antifa and for these neo-Nazis to be there."

Antifa practically burned down cities like Portland and Seattle. It's why President Trump declared them a terrorist organization in 2020. Yet here we had prime-time anchors defending the violence and destruction they inflicted on the public. Incredible.

This hard pivot to the left was not lost on John Malone, the largest shareholder of Discovery, which purchased CNN from AT&T in 2022.

"I would like to see CNN evolve back to the kind of journalism that it started with, and actually have journalists, which would be unique and refreshing," Malone said during a CNBC interview.

Malone was advocating for a nonpartisan news network, something CNN had been before. Commonsense stuff. And if the network could bring back some Republican and independent viewers, the reasoning went, that kind of wider net would be good for business.

Stelter, who really believed he was indispensable despite having a program that was pummeled on a weekly basis by Fox's *Media Buzz*, publicly took exception:

"The people who say the Zucker-era CNN was lacking in real journalism clearly were not watching CNN directly. My best guess is that they were watching talking heads and reading columnists complain about CNN. And yes, I'm including John Malone in this."

The hubris that Michael Wolff talked about was again on full display. Stelter was fired a few months later. Some media analysts said the ouster was because the network was moving back to the center, and Stelter's bias would hinder that effort. That's true. But when your senior media guy attempts to undermine new management from within, both publicly and behind the scenes, there is no choice but to remove him . . . like a cancerous tumor.

On cue, Stelter was almost immediately hired by Harvard, another school I'll never pay to send my kids to. They brought him on to teach a course on (checks notes) the dangers of misinformation.

Given that Harvard hired the worst mayor in the history of mayors, Bill de Blasio of New York City, to be a professor, as well as former mayor Lori Lightfoot, the second-worst mayor in the history of my beloved Chicago, Stelter is surely fitting right in.

Back to CNN, the problem for Chris Licht was that Jeff Zucker loyalists never accepted him as the new boss. Everything came to a head when Licht hosted the leading candidate for the 2024 Republican presidential nomination on the network in a town hall program in May 2023.

Having Donald Trump as a candidate on CNN was not exactly a foreign concept. CNN held several town halls for him back in 2015–16. In fact, Zucker's CNN covered almost all of Trump's rallies in full, and even showed empty podiums of upcoming Trump speeches with chyrons stating "Awaiting Donald Trump Speech." And ratings went through the roof for the network during that election season, with CNN capturing its highest viewership in network history.

So Licht had his marching orders: ask more Republicans to come on the network; ask tough questions of members of both parties and treat them fairly. Trump received 74 million votes in 2020, the most ever for a Republican presidential candidate in history. At the time of the town hall, he was up by more than 30 points in the RealClearPolitics average of major polls over Gov. Ron DeSantis (R-FL) for the GOP nomination.

What should CNN have done—pretended he didn't exist?

After the Trump town hall with Kaitlin Collins on May 23, 2023, the left showed its outrage, both from outside the network but from inside it, too, and even somehow on its own air.

"*The man you were so disturbed to see last night*, that man is the front-runner for the Republican nomination for president," anchor Anderson Cooper told viewers the following night. "And I get it. It was disturbing."

"You have every right to be outraged today, angry, and never watch this network again," he later added.

Imagine you're the president of an international news network, and you're watching someone who is supposed to be your top anchor telling viewers not to watch while assuming *all* were "disturbed" by the sight of a former president the network used to worship from a ratings perspective.

Before he knew it, Licht's entire morning editorial calls were being leaked verbatim to people like Stelter, while his in-house media newsletter reported that he had "alienated much of the employee base and squandered the goodwill" he had when he took the helm of the network.

This isn't to say Licht hasn't had his share of screwups. The biggest—and arguably most surprising—occurred when he decided to move Don Lemon, then the lowest-rated prime-time host among the Big Three in cable news (Fox News, MSNBC, CNN), to mornings, pairing him with Collins and Poppy Harlow. It was a disaster: *CNN This Morning* launched in November, and within six months Lemon, continually embroiled in controversy, got fired while Collins was moved to 9:00 p.m., leaving only Harlow as an original cast member. The show struggles to attract more than four hundred thousand viewers despite reaching more than eighty million homes.

An unflattering profile of Licht in the *Atlantic* sealed his fate—not so much because of Licht's attempt to rearrange the deck chairs on the *Titanic*, but because of his view of the network's coverage of Covid under Zucker.

"In the beginning it was a trusted source—this crazy thing, no one understands it, help us make sense of it. What's going on?" Licht said. "And I think then it got to a place where, 'Oh wow, we gotta keep getting those ratings. We gotta keep getting the sense of urgency.'

"People walked outside and they go, 'This is not my life. This is not my reality. You guys are just saying this because you need the ratings, you need the clicks. I don't trust you,'" he added.

An internal survey commissioned by the network, first reported by Semafor in June 2023, found that viewers gave CNN low marks in terms of trustworthiness regarding its Covid coverage, which included a running total of deaths in what critics called "the Death Clock" that played on fear. (Curiously, the Death Clock went away shortly after Joe Biden took office, despite there being more Covid deaths in 2021 than 2020.)

CNN's inmates had successfully carried out a mutiny in broad daylight. None had learned anything about their own flaws. Because here's why so many people have such disdain for the network: their anchors all insist they're serious journalists and not opinion hosts. The following juxtaposition sums up why that's complete bullshit.

"I'm not an opinion host. I'm talking to people from different sides and trying to be straight down the middle and represent things fairly and accurately. I keep my head down. I just try to do the best I can," Anderson Cooper once declared in September 2023.

If Cooper doesn't give opinions, what would one call this exactly?

"That is the president of the United States," Cooper said in 2020 after playing a clip from Trump. "That is the most powerful person in the world, and we see him like an obese turtle on his back flailing in the hot sun, realizing his time is over, but he just hasn't accepted it, and he wants to take everybody down with him, including this country."

An obese turtle. That was obviously rehearsed and loaded for the sole purpose of going viral, which it did.

But remember, Cooper isn't an opinion host, right? And this is where CNN misread the room throughout the Trump years as ratings relatively soared: people didn't tune in to hear what Cooper or Lemon or Stelter were *feeling* on a particular night or morning. They wanted news, especially that of the truly breaking variety.

One of the few holdovers from the old days of CNN is Wolf Blitzer. Wolf isn't exactly Mr. Personality, but as a true news anchor, that doesn't necessarily have to be in the DNA. Blitzer didn't do screeds and still doesn't engage in that behavior in the way Stelter did and Jake Tapper still does. He never tried to draw attention to himself the way Chris Cuomo did when he infamously faked his own Covid quarantine in 2020. Yet viewers still had affection for Wolf because he was trusted and had a certain AI quirkiness to him. This affection even led to his being chosen to appear on *Celebrity Jeopardy!*, where he finished $4,600 in debt while Conan O'Brien's sidekick Andy Richter racked up $68,000 in winnings.

When Donald Trump came on the scene in 2015, CNN's ratings exploded. The network's biggest rating, to this day, was when it hosted the second GOP presidential primary debate and attracted twenty-four million viewers. Its other biggest rating moments were Election Night of 2016, Election Night of 2020, and January 6, 2021.

Summary: As evidenced by the plunge in ratings starting in 2021, no one was tuning in because they needed to hear the DNC-approved opinions of its anchors; they were tuning in for what the news cycle was providing, not the people telling us how to think.

Chris Licht, the wunderkind behind MSNBC's *Morning Joe* and *Late Night with Stephen Colbert*, was looking for work again—all because his own staff had turned on him for having the audacity to not be left-leaning enough.

Of course, the coup against Licht was something that had been un-folding since basically the first day he took the reins at CNN. The knives were out not so much for Licht himself on a personal level but for the mission: getting back to the Zucker era of being the resistance network to Donald Trump and anyone who supports him on the right. In other words, MSNBC 2.0.

In the summer of 2023, Mark Thompson, the former chief at the *New York Times*, was tapped to replace Licht. Given how liberal the *Times* is, Thompson will likely keep the inmates happy by not attempt-ing another move to the center. If he does, he'll have to deal with the likes of Christiane Amanpour, yet another anchor who fancies herself an actual journalist.

"I want to do what's right and empathize with and acknowledge all those who need to trust us at CNN, the most trusted name in news. I understand that the town hall a week ago was for many an earthquake," the condescending Amanpour told Columbia University graduates in May 2023 after the Trump town hall. "The fact that the American people voted three times against Trump and Trumpism—2018, 2020, 2022—also speaks volumes. We've done our duty, we've told the story, we have put that in everybody's awareness and people have had the opportunity to make their choices and they have done."

We've done our duty. How's that? Because Trump lost—*that* was the mission? The duty? Of pushing the Steele dossier? Trump-Russian collusion?

In January 2024, Donald Trump won the Iowa caucus by more than four touchdowns (30 points) over Ron DeSantis and by 32 points over Nikki Haley. As any news organization would do, CNN cut to Donald Trump's victory speech, where the former president talked about the number one issue for Iowans according to exit polls: illegal immigration and the border.

"Anchor" Jake Tapper, however, was having none of this. Allow Trump to speak to voters across the country directly and without a filter about a top issue? That wasn't going to happen. So in the most sanctimonious and dishonest manner possible, Tapper cut in.

Trump: "Right now we have an invasion. We have an invasion of millions and millions of people that are coming into our country. I can't imagine why they think that's a good thing."

Tapper: "Donald Trump declaring victory with a historically strong showing in the Iowa caucuses. If these numbers hold the biggest victory for a non-incumbent president in the modern era for this contest, a relatively subdued speech as these things go so far, although here he is right now under, under my voice. You hear him repeating his anti-immigrant rhetoric."

What a farce. For starters, Trump wasn't engaging in "anti-immigrant rhetoric." He was talking about illegal immigration to the tune of millions at the US border and what it was doing to the country. But Tapper purposely omitted the illegal part in an effort to paint Trump as a xenophobic racist.

Again, this was the same network that showed almost all of Trump's rallies live during the 2016 campaign because they loved the ratings and buzz that came with it. But now, suddenly, Trump cannot be shown live to viewers. This is the same network that bear-hugs Adam Schiff in every interview. And the same network that practically had a cot in its green rooms for Michael Avenatti during his heyday, and even had its media reporter at the time declare he had a chance to win the presidency.

On that night in Iowa, CNN never went back to Trump's speech. Instead, they offered the usual political panel the size of an NBA roster to give their take on Trump with almost nothing positive or objective to offer. And when ratings came out the next day, the scoreboard showed Fox averaging 2.5 million viewers, nearly quadrupling those of CNN, which averaged under 675,000 viewers.

Yep. Great strategy. Keep it up.

"I think they're stickin' with politics a little too much," Ted Turner, the man who founded and launched CNN in 1980, told Ted Koppel in a rare 2018 interview. "They—they'd do better to have—a more balanced—agenda."

From Ted's lips to God's ears . . .

Such is the state of media in the twenty-first century. It's a scary time for free speech in the country whose greatness was built on it.

EPILOGUE

Hey, folks! Many, many thanks for reading the book. I've said this in interviews and will reiterate here: if you told me even in my thirties that I had the ability to crank out nearly seventy thousand words all on my own (no ghostwriters or outside researchers were used for this book), I would have said you were as crazy as Sunny Hostin.

I've been a reporter and columnist for years, but that usually requires just a thousand or fifteen hundred words. Think of a 200-meter dash versus a marathon, and I was definitely not a marathoner, at least until now. And here we are: two books down! And while *Come On, Man! The Truth about Joe Biden's Terrible, Horrible, No-Good, Very Bad Presidency* was fun to write, this offering truly was a labor of love, because it was such an eye-opener regarding just how perilous things are in this country in 2024.

Like you, I just cannot fathom how major cities like Chicago and San Francisco keep electing Democrat mayors who clearly don't have the best interests of their citizens in mind. I can't get my head around spending trillions of dollars we don't have, and why balanced-budget amendments aren't etched in stone. I definitely do not know how this administration can continue to allow millions into this country unabated, although the goal is clear: to make them future voters, even if some are terrorists looking to harm this country the way Hamas harmed Israel. They simply do not care. It's all about power. It's all about control. Same goes for the teachers' unions, who don't remotely care about your child's education, only power. Only control.

Per my friends at Pew Research, trust in the government is near a *seventy-year low*. Just one in seven American adults say they trust the federal government. *One in seven*. Two-thirds say they always or often feel "exhausted" when it comes to politics. And the top two words they use to describe politics in this country? *Divisive* and *corrupt*. I'd throw in *immature* as well, and that goes for many members on both sides of the aisle, who exist for likes, retweets, and going on cable news.

As for the media, it's not even a question anymore about the institution being hopelessly biased. There are very few real journalists left. It's dominated by the hacktivists. Yet some still insist there is no bias. Really.

"The Republicans have been running on, 'There's a liberal bias in the media.' If you say something long enough, there are liberals who say there's a liberal bias in the media when you see polling now," Chuck Todd said on *Meet the Press*. And he was as serious as a heart attack.

"The Republicans have subsumed all of this, and it's turned into this. We should have fought back better in the mainstream media. We shouldn't [have] accepted the premise that there was liberal bias. We should have defended," he added.

Defended what? The fact that NBC News covered Trump negatively 93 percent of the time? And remember what the Trump presidency was for the first three years before Covid upended the country: The United States was enjoying one of its greatest economic stretches in history. Our border was relatively secure. We were energy independent. NAFTA out, Trump's vastly better United States–Mexico–Canada Agreement in. And we were at peace. Yet most of our media branded Trump as the worst president ever.

Given where we are now, with open borders, inflation tripled, wages not keeping up with inflation, crime completely out of control, our education system failing our kids while we're getting our clocks cleaned by China, and the world in what feels like perpetual war, would you take America in 2019 again? How about America in 1997 under a sensible Democrat like Bill Clinton?

Rhetorical questions.

Instead, we're currently governed by Barack Obama's JV team and perhaps even by Obama himself behind the scenes. Everything feels hopeless. The optimism the United States once had is no more.

That is why the upcoming election means absolutely everything. This version of the Democratic Party must lose. This kind of governing and philosophy cannot be rewarded. The only way that party will ever stop going further and further left is if they lose, and lose big. For if they don't, and it bears repeating, conservatives may lose power permanently after Puerto Rico and Washington, DC, become states (instantly creating four permanent Democrat senators), the Supreme Court is expanded until there is a liberal majority, voting becomes federalized to rig the process in the Democrats' favor, and the Electoral College is eliminated, all with a corrupt media pushing their initiatives to save democracy. Or something.

Unfortunately, the days of compromise may be gone forever. There will be no more moments when Ronald Reagan hashed out differences over a stiff drink. There will be no more Democrats like Clinton getting meaningful things done with a Newt Gingrich. This is war, plain and simple. And wars aren't won until the opposition is decisively and thoroughly crushed and common sense is common again. This isn't about rooting for Republicans or Democrats or conservatives or liberals. My team is common sense. Logic. Pragmatism. Is that too much to ask for?

If you see me on TV or hear me on the radio, however, you know that I'm generally a happy guy who doesn't take himself remotely seriously, so let's end this sucker on a bright note with a story about my eight-year-old son and ten-year-old daughter.

My wife and I had decided we weren't going to name either of our kids until they left the womb (her womb, to be clear; I know you can't assume these days) and we could get a good look at them. Sometimes even babies just look like a certain name. Cameron was an easy name to agree to. But when Liam was born two years later, on August 28, 2015, Jean and I weren't on the same page.

Doctor (while holding the baby up): *Congratulations! It's a boy!*

Me (looking down below his waist in awe): *Wow! And what a boy!*

Doctor: *No, sir. That's the umbilical cord. You have to cut that . . .*

Me: *D'oh!*

Jean: *I think we're looking at a Liam, babe.*

Me: *Well, Liam is a nice name. Classic Irish name, sure. But I'm looking at that jawline, those eyes, and . . . let's go . . . let's go Brandon!*

Jean: *I don't know . . . I got a real bad feeling about that name.*

She was prophetic. Imagine having a kid named Brandon. Even worse, could you also imagine if we named Cameron . . . *Karen* instead?

OK. I can see that you're smiling. This is a good way to end the book. Thanks again for reading!

ACKNOWLEDGMENTS

J ust wanted to throw out some big thank-yous to everyone who helped make this book possible.

Thanks to the great team at HarperCollins and Broadside Books for being just about the easiest folks one can possibly collaborate with. Professional. Meticulous. Amiable.

Thanks to Fox News for allowing me the airtime to promote it and for your ongoing support throughout my career.

Most of all, thanks to my family for all your positive thoughts and ideas on this one.

INDEX

ABOUT THE AUTHOR

JOE CONCHA was born and raised in the swamps of New Jersey. The husband of Jean and the father of Cameron and Liam, he enjoys baseball, the beach, and his many leather-bound books. He is a Fox News contributor and a media and political columnist. His previous book, *Come On, Man!*, is one of the bestselling books about Joe Biden published since 2020.